SELECTED CLIMBS:

MONT BLANC & THE AIGUILLES ROUGES

60 ROCK ROUTES FROM F4 TO F6a+

THE AUTHORS

Jean-Louis Laroche is a mountain guide, freelance photographer, journalist and guidebook writer. He has spent more than thirty years exploring the Mont Blanc Massif and during this time he has climbed all the area's classic routes, made first ascents of numerous ice climbs and trodden many of the world's most beautiful mountains.

Florence Lelong shares her love of the natural environment through her work as a freelance photographer, illustrator, hiking guide and mountaineer. She has co-written numerous books and guidebooks and regularly contributes work to the press, news agencies and publishers. Laroche and Lelong are also authors of *Mountaineering in the Mont Blanc Range* (Vertebrate Publishing, 2014), and run the *Alpinisme-Escalades* climbing school.

We would like to thank the following people for their invaluable help: Alain Alfidéo, Evelyne and Pierre Allain, Patrick Bachet, Myriam Boucher, Iain Cleaver, Didier Cottard, François Damilano, Janos and Paulo Dudas, Patrick Gabarrou, Yves Ghesquiers, Stéphanie Guinée, Théo Laroche, Anne Lison, Jean-Marie Ollivier, Lionel Pernollet, Régis Philippe and the staff of the Office de Haute Montagne.

Cover photo: The Rébuffat route on the Aiguille du Midi.
Back cover photo: Tour Ronde, Mont Blanc and the spires of the Tacul in the heart of the Vallée Blanche.

Photography by Jean-Louis Laroche and Florence Lelong (except page 69, by Jean-Marie Ollivier).
Diagrams by Florence Lelong (except the map on page 5 and the topo on page 93).
'Montagne-Évasion' collection edited by Pascal Sombardier.

First published in 2009 by Éditions Glénat.

Title of the original French edition:
Escalades choisies - Mont-Blanc Aiguilles Rouges

This English language edition first published in 2015 in the UK, Europe, India, South Africa, Australia and New Zealand by Vertebrate Publishing.

Vertebrate Publishing
Crescent House, 228 Psalter Lane, Sheffield S11 8UT.
www.v-publishing.co.uk

All trade enquiries in the UK, Europe and Commonwealth (except Canada) to:
Cordee, 11 Jacknell Road, Dodwells Bridge Industrial Estate, Hinckley, LE10 3BS, UK.
www.cordee.co.uk

ISBN: 978-1-910240-45-8

Translated from the French by Paul Henderson (traduction@paulhenderson.fr).

Produced by Rod Harrison, Vertebrate Graphics Ltd,
based on an original design by Éditions Glénat. - www.v-graphics.co.uk

Printed in EU by Pulsio SARL.

SELECTED CLIMBS:

MONT BLANC & THE AIGUILLES ROUGES

60 ROCK ROUTES FROM F4 TO F6a+

Jean-Louis Laroche & Florence Lelong

Translated by Paul Henderson

Vertebrate Publishing, Sheffield

www.v-publishing.co.uk

CONTENTS

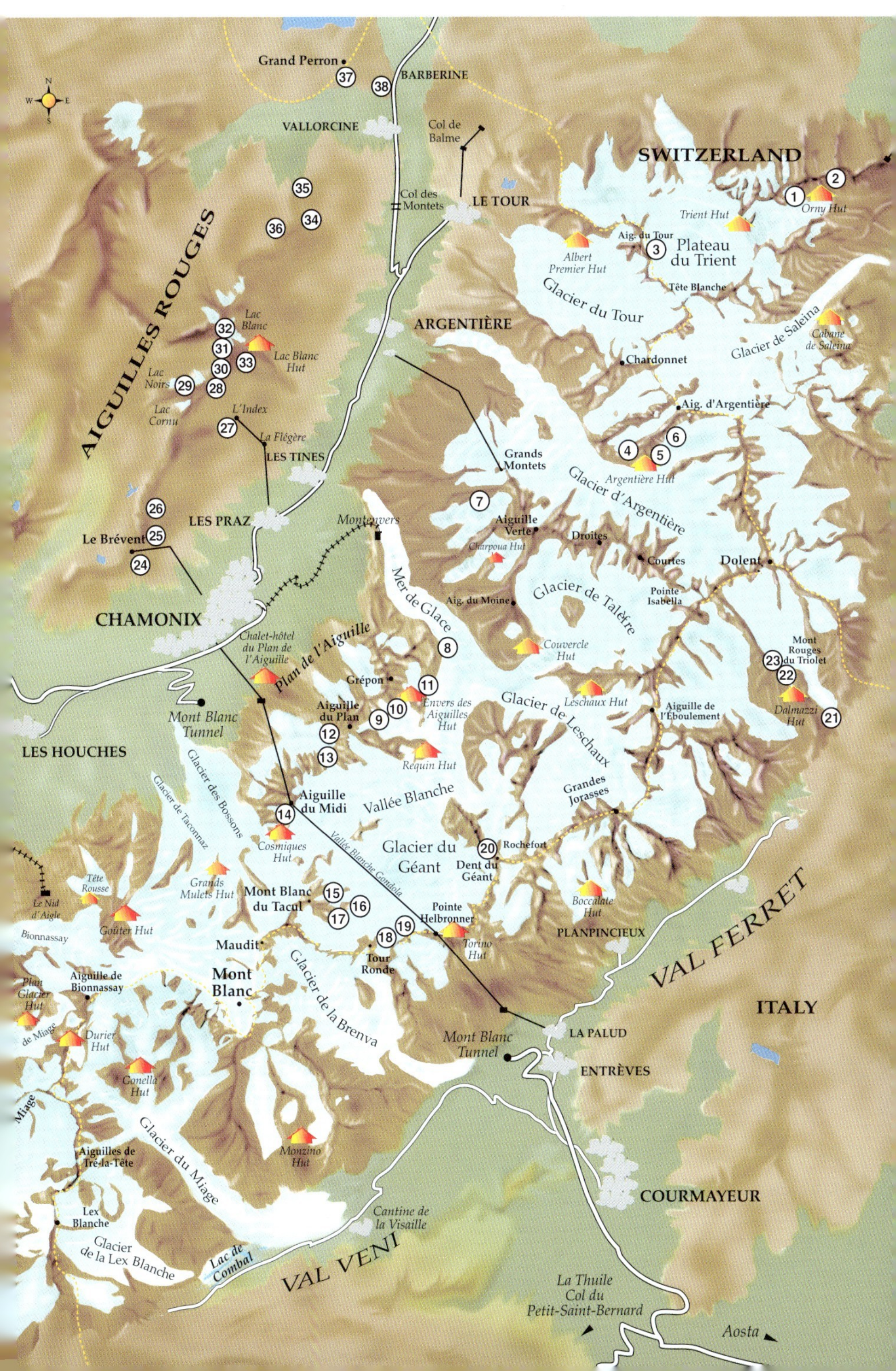

Grand Perron
BARBERINE
VALLORCINE
Col de Balme
SWITZERLAND
Col des Montets
LE TOUR
Trient Hut
Orny Hut
Aig. du Tour
Albert Premier Hut
Plateau du Trient
AIGUILLES ROUGES
Glacier du Tour
Tête Blanche
ARGENTIÈRE
Cabane de Saleina
Glacier de Saleina
Lac Blanc
Lac Blanc Hut
Chardonnet
Lac Noirs
Aig. d'Argentière
Lac Cornu
L'Index
La Flégère
LES TINES
Grands Montets
Argentière Hut
Glacier d'Argentière
LES PRAZ
Montenvers
Aiguille Verte
Le Brévent
Droites
Charpoua Hut
Courtes
Dolent
Mer de Glace
Aig. du Moine
Glacier de Talèfre
Pointe Isabella
CHAMONIX
Chalet-hôtel du Plan de l'Aiguille
Plan de l'Aiguille
Couvercle Hut
Mont Rouges du Triolet
Grépon
Envers des Aiguilles Hut
Leschaux Hut
Mont Blanc Tunnel
Aiguille du Plan
Glacier de Leschaux
Aiguille de l'Éboulement
Dalmazzi Hut
LES HOUCHES
Requin Hut
Glacier des Bossons
Glacier de Taconnaz
Aiguille du Midi
Vallée Blanche
Grandes Jorasses
Cosmiques Hut
Vallée Blanche Gondola
Glacier du Géant
Rochefort
Tête Rousse
Grands Mulets Hut
Dent du Géant
Le Nid d'Aigle
Mont Blanc du Tacul
Boccalate Hut
Goûter Hut
Pointe Helbronner
Bionnassay
Maudit
Torino Hut
PLANPINCIEUX
Tour Ronde
Mont Blanc
Aiguille de Bionnassay
Glacier de la Brenva
VAL FERRET
Plan Glacier Hut
ITALY
de Miage
Durier Hut
Mont Blanc Tunnel
LA PALUD
ENTRÈVES
Gonella Hut
Miage
Glacier du Miage
Monzino Hut
Aiguilles de Tré-la-Tête
COURMAYEUR
Lex Blanche
Cantine de la Visaille
Glacier de la Lex Blanche
Lac de Combal
VAL VENI
La Thuile Col du Petit-Saint-Bernard
Aosta
N
S
E
W

INTRODUCTION

Climbing has changed a lot over the last few decades. Year-round training, both indoors and outdoors, has led to a huge increase in standards and the search for 'recreational' climbs. As a result, our selection in this book focuses on enjoyable climbs with easy access and descents, rejecting routes with sections of poor climbing, difficult or dangerous approaches, or that are very long or always in the shade. All the routes here can be climbed in one day, generally carrying only a very small rucksack.

Our selection of sixty climbs on forty summits in seventeen areas includes established classics and recent additions, and covers a variety of rock types (gneiss and granite), climbing styles (slabs, corners, steep walls) and protection (bolts, pegs, nuts, cams). The rating system should enable regular climbers to choose routes suited to their abilities and to decide between climbs that can be tackled in a leisurely fashion and those requiring a more efficient approach, although none of the routes described are excessively committing.

In order to ensure ratings are as accurate and consistent as possible, we sought a consensus from several aficionados of the massif's rock routes. In the very small number of cases where opinions as to the correct rating differed, we chose the grade that was most coherent with the grading of the other routes in order to ensure grades are compatible between the different areas.

In recent years, the Aiguilles Rouges has been the 'in place' to climb, thanks to a new-routing boom that has touched almost every climbable outcrop. This has resulted in a large number of pleasant, middle-grade climbs with easy walk-ins that can be done in half a day. Many of these routes are close to ski lifts; others are in more remote corners of the massif where mankind has had almost no visible impact on the landscape.

It can take a little time to get used to climbing on the gneiss of the Aiguille Rouges, due to its sometimes-shiny surface, sloping holds and little edges – rather than jugs – and the steepness of some sections of the routes.

Climbing in the Mont Blanc Massif offers a completely different experience in a magnificent setting whose two most important characteristics are the glaciated terrain and the altitude. As a result, conditions are much more variable (amount of snow cover, size and position of crevasses and bergschrunds). An ice axe and crampons will often be needed to get to the routes, especially for approaches across glaciers, where it is recommended to rope up.

In order to reduce the difficulties due to the high-altitude environment, we have chosen only routes of moderate length with relatively easy approaches, sunny aspects and, often, abseil descents. Nevertheless, it is essential to be able to place natural protection to complement any *in situ* bolts and pegs.

If you have the time, it may be worthwhile spending several nights in a hut in order to make the best of the walk in. In spring, the easiest way to get to some routes may be on touring skis because, until proven otherwise, snow 'springs eternal'. Finally, is it necessary to once again extol the purity of the rock, this wonderful granite, burning gold in the crystal-clear air of the high mountains?

Left: Third tower on the *Papillons Ridge* (6a).

Opposite page: *Marchand de Sable*, the perfect slab.

PRACTICAL INFORMATION

MAPS

All the climbs described in this guidebook are within the area covered by the 1:25,000 IGN TOP 25 map for Chamonix (3630 OT). The contour interval is 10m in France and Italy, 20m in Switzerland.

START POINT

The car park, hut or lift from which the climb is reached. Descriptions of access routes to the huts and information about ski lifts are given on pages 94–95.

DIFFICULTY

Each route is rated in terms of its overall difficulty and the technical difficulty of the hardest moves on the route. Where appropriate, two technical grades are given, one for the hardest moves for an entirely free ascent and one for the hardest moves that cannot be avoided by using aid (indicated by the term 'oblig.' for obligatory).

For example: D+, 6a, 5c oblig. refers to a route whose overall difficulty is D+, with a 6a crux that can be avoided by using aid, thereby reducing the technical difficulty to 5c.

Overall difficulty is indicated using the alpine grading system, which takes into account route length, altitude, commitment, difficulty of the approach (for example, snow slope or glacier) and descent (complexity, difficult abseils), number of difficult pitches (sustained nature of the climbing, boldness), state of any *in situ* protection and ease of retreat, and so on. The routes described in this guidebook fall within the categories: **AD (Quite Difficult)**, **D (Difficult)** and **TD (Very Difficult)**. Routes at the top end or bottom end of their category are indicated by the suffixes **+** and **–** (for example, **AD+**, **TD-**).

The technical difficulty of the climbing, taking into account the need to be able to place natural protection (nuts, cams, slings), is expressed using a numerical grade from **1 to 9**. Subdivisions within each numerical grade are indicated by the letters **a**, **b**, **c**, and the suffix + (for example, **6a**, **6a+**, **6b**, **6b+**, and so on.).

The grade **A0** indicates a section of easy aid climbing that can be overcome by pulling on the *in situ* gear.

Left: On *Les Violons Tziganes.*

Below: Théo training hard.

Tour Ronde, Mont Blanc and the spires of the Tacul in the heart of the Vallée Blanche.

GLACIER APPROACHES

The approaches to most of the routes in the Mont Blanc Massif involve crossing glaciers. Routes across glaciers can only be indicative, as conditions vary throughout the season and from year to year (number of crevasses, snow slopes that become bare ice, size of bergschrunds).

There are no glaciers in the Aiguilles Rouges but it may be necessary to cross snowfields or climb snow-filled gullies to get to some routes at the beginning of the season.

TIMES AND VERTICAL HEIGHT

Times are averages for rope teams in which both climbers have the ability and experience required for the chosen route.

All the routes can be climbed in one day.

The vertical height is the difference in elevation between the foot of the route and the summit. This distance may not always correspond to the altitudes marked on the map.

CONDITIONS

In addition to a recommended season, we have noted specific details for each cliff (for example, if a climb is slow to dry after rain).

GEAR

Basic rock climbing gear.

Climbing shoes, two 50m ropes, descender, eight to twelve quickdraws, four to six extra karabiners, slings of various lengths, one set of nuts, cams 1–3.5, helmet.

Plus: food and drink for on the route, first aid kit, head torch, radio, warm clothing for routes at altitude.

- Crampons and ice axe if the approach crosses snowfields (for example, early in the season) or glaciers. Climbers are advised to rope up and to carry crevasse rescue gear when crossing glaciers.
- Any specific gear that may be required is described in the relevant chapter.

AIGUILLE D'ORNY (3,167M)

SOUTH-WEST FACE: CLASSIC ROUTE

START POINT: Orny Hut (2,811m) in Switzerland. Reached in 2 hrs by taking the Breya chairlift from Champex. See pages 94–95.

DIFFICULTY: D, 5a oblig. Sustained and varied. *In situ* belays and protection on the cruxes. Complex route finding.

TIMES: approach 40 mins; climb 3 hrs; descent 1 hr back to the hut.

VERTICAL HEIGHT: 200m.

CONDITIONS: June to September (snow patches can remain well into spring).

GEAR: short ice axe at the beginning of the season (approach and descent), nuts, cams 1–3.5.

FIRST ASCENT: unknown. Bolted by Raymond Angeloz.

The Orny Hut is surrounded by superb climbs of all styles and all grades, so it is worth going up for several days. In addition, most of the routes can be reached without going on to the glacier. A route book full of information can be found in the hut's dining room.

Providing well-protected climbing on perfect, buff-coloured rock high above the glacier, the *Classic Route* on the Aiguille d'Orny's south-west face is a great introduction to longer rock routes. Beyond the first pitch, novices will start to get a feel for the immensity of the face and the logic of the line, following natural weaknesses, guided by the *in situ* gear, as they work their way to the summit.

APPROACH

From the hut, a good path leads westwards below the single-pitch climbs. Contour across the cirque below the Col d'Arpette, noting the descent gully as you go past (the furthest left of the three gullies opposite the hut). Go over a shoulder, then go up the scree slope or snowfield below the south-west face of the Aiguille d'Orny, aiming for the foot of the gully to the left of the face (enormous jammed block). 40 mins.

DESCENT

A 20m abseil from a ring bolt on the east face, 10m below the summit, leads to a muddy ledge. Go along this ledge for 50m, then descend the south-east slope (scree or snow) to the horizontal ridge on the left (east) side of the slope. Head south along the ridge to two large cairns at the top of a steep gully (200m) above the hut. Go down this gully, then follow the path below the Col d'Arpette back to the hut. 1 hr.

The *Classic Route* on the south-west face, high above the Glacier d'Orny.

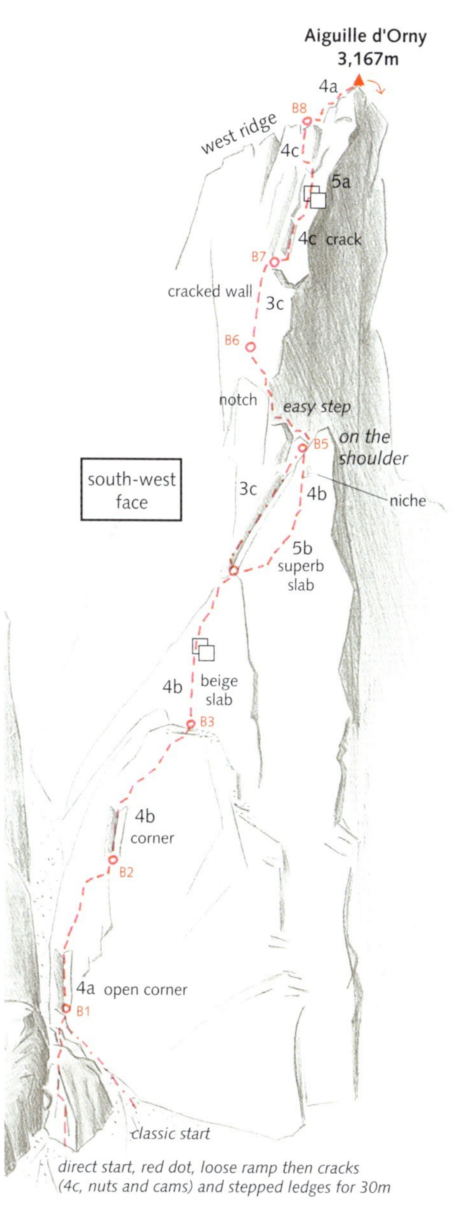

At the start of the route, looking across to the Grand Combin.

AIGUILLE DE LA CABANE (2,999M)

SOUTH FACE: BON ACCUEIL

START POINT: Orny Hut (2,811m) in Switzerland. Reached in 2 hrs by taking the Breya chairlift from Champex. See pages 94–95.

DIFFICULTY: D-, 4c oblig. Slabs and steep cracks. *In situ* belays and protection on the cruxes.

TIMES: approach 20 mins; route 2 hrs; descent 1 hr.

VERTICAL HEIGHT: 180m.

CONDITIONS: relatively low altitude, so often in condition in spring.

GEAR: basic set of nuts and cams.

FIRST ASCENT: C. & Y. Rémy, 7 July 1986.

The Aiguille de la Cabane is so close to the hut that it can be climbed on the same day as the walk in. Of the four routes on the steep but juggy rock of the south face, *Bon Accueil* is the most varied. Its two great highlights are the exposed ridge of the lower buttress, and the summit tower, split by a perfect corner that gives highly elegant climbing. *Namaste* (5c) is the face's other gem and an excellent choice as a second route.

The descent – an integral part of every climb – will call upon your route-finding skills, as it goes down a different face. It is worth noting a few landmarks during the walk in.

The crux: 5c, steep but with good holds.

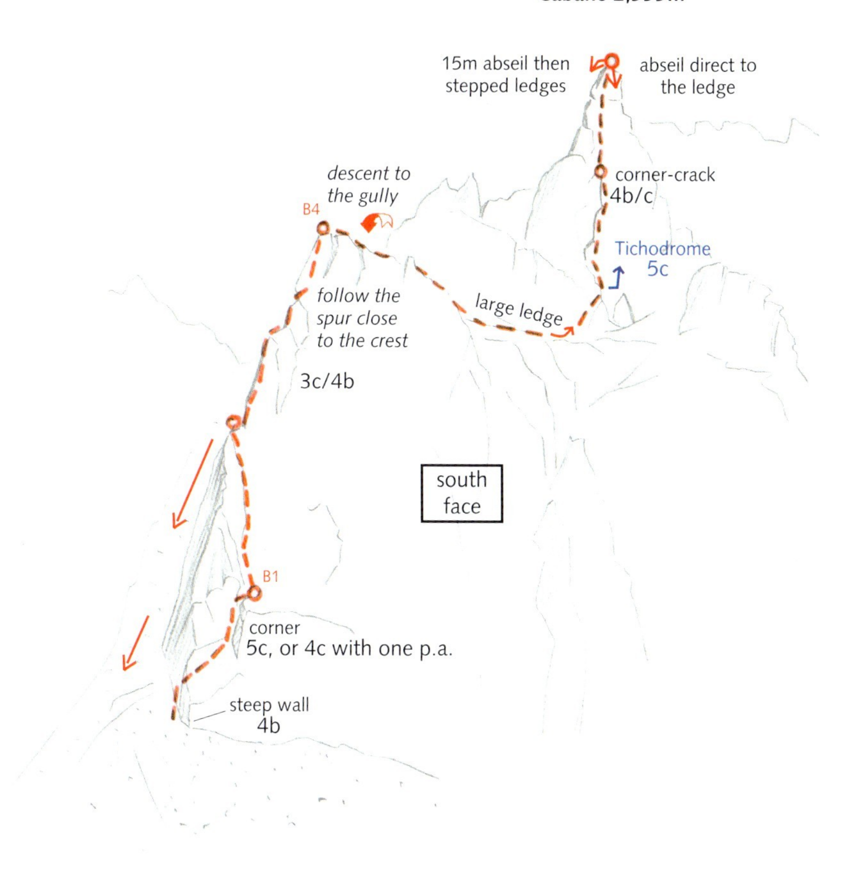

APPROACH

Head north-west up the scree slopes above the hut to the foot of the spur on the right-hand edge of the descent gully. 20 mins. The route starts just right of the gully (large red dot).

DESCENT

(a) Either abseil back down to the large ledge (50m), then head right (west) up the ledge to a small saddle and descend the south-west-facing gully below.

(b) Or abseil down the west face (15m) to the foot of the summit tower, then head west down stepped ledges. Go left (south) round the secondary pinnacles to get to the saddle at the top of the descent gully.

AIGUILLE PURTSCHELLER (3,478M)

CLASSIC SOUTH RIDGE

START POINT: Albert Premier (1er) Hut (2,702m, 1½ hrs from the Col de Balme) or Trient Hut (3,170m, 3 hrs from Champex in Switzerland via the Breya chairlift). See pages 94–95.
DIFFICULTY: D+, 5a oblig. Quite sustained, sometimes strenuous and with one short bold section. Nut and cam protection. Glacier approach.
TIMES: approach 2 hrs (1 hr from Trient); climb 2hrs; abseils 1 hr; return to hut 1 hr.
VERTICAL HEIGHT: 150m.
CONDITIONS: spring (approach on skis) to autumn.
GEAR: crampons, ice axes, ice screws, long slings, nuts, cams 1–3.
FIRST ASCENT: R. Aubert, R. Dittert & F. Marullaz, 16 May 1943.

In this area, where most of the routes are glacier climbs, excellent rock routes of a reasonable length are rare. One exception to this rule is the Aiguille Purtscheller, whose superb rough granite is a delight to climb on.

A glacier approach, complex route finding, a little exposure, sometimes strenuous climbing, and an abseil descent on the north face combine to provide a superbly varied day out. It is also a great way of testing your skills before tackling more ambitious climbs.

APPROACH

Follow the path east from the Albert Premier Hut (boulders, snow, cairns) to the Glacier du Tour (20 mins). Go up the glacier and around the north side of the Signal Reilly (2,883m). Head south-east up a steep slope, then follow the 3,100m contour until just past the west ridge of the Purtscheller. Head due east up the wide gully below the Col Supérieur du Tour (3,289m). Just after the col, turn left and aim for an obvious V-notch, reached by crossing the bergschrund and climbing a short snow slope. 2 hrs from the hut.

DESCENT

From the summit belay, climb down the north face for 8m to the first abseil station. Three abseils down the right bank (20m, 35m and 50m) lead almost to the Col Purtscheller. From here, follow the Glacier du Trient past the foot of the east face of the Aiguille Purtscheller to the Col Supérieur du Tour. Follow the approach track back to the hut (2 hrs from the summit).

Note: It is possible to follow the crest of the ridge at a slightly higher grade (TD-).

The 5a slab above the V-notch.

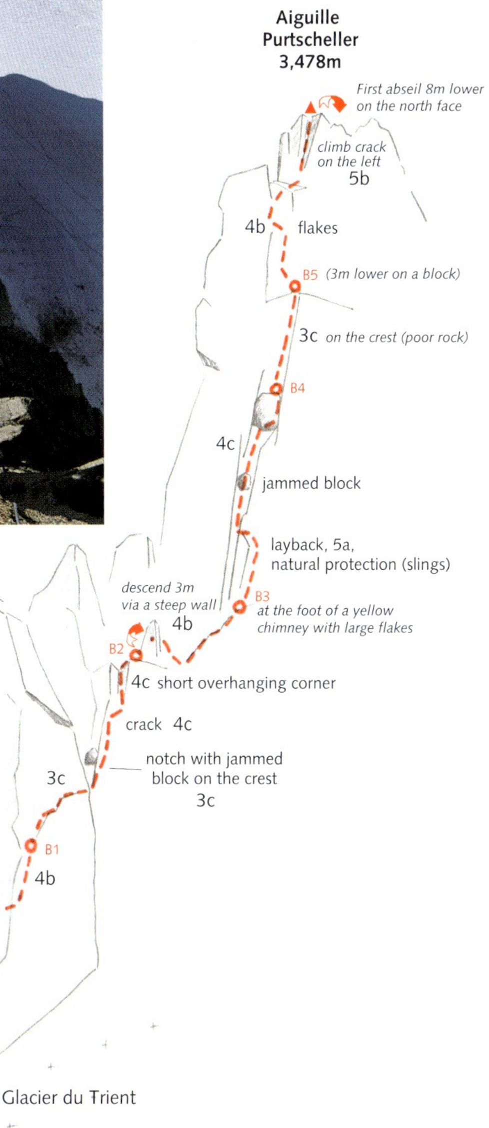

PLATEAU DU JARDIN (3,177M)

SOUTH FACE: CENTRAL CORNER

START POINT: Argentière Hut (2,771m), 1½ hrs from the top of the Grands Montets cable car. See pages 94–95.

DIFFICULTY: TD, 6a oblig. Sustained. Steep corners and cracks with natural protection. Abseil descent from B6. Can continue to the Plateau, but the descent via the Améthystes face is long and complex.

TIMES: approach 30 mins; climb 4 hrs; descent abseil from B6 45 mins; walk off from summit 1½ hrs.

VERTICAL HEIGHT: 300m.

CONDITIONS: exposed to westerly storms and slow to dry.

GEAR: nuts, two sets of cams 0.5–3.5.

FIRST ASCENT: R. Ravanel & F. Simatos, August 1972.

Big north faces are not the only climbs to be found in the Argentière Basin. The Plateau is one of several minor summits above the hut whose sunny walls are equipped for abseil descents. Lying at the foot of the Glacier du Milieu, just above the Aiguille d'Argentière normal route, the area has panache and the clean-cut corner that bisects the face is quite demanding. Climbers must have the skill and confidence to place gear in the six-pitch crack and the crux requires reading the rock quickly in order to link the moves while placing protection.

Exiting on to the Plateau, rather than abseiling down the route, takes you into a corner of the massif that is as untamed as it was in the days of the pioneers.

APPROACH

Head north-west along the path from the hut to the Glacier du Milieu and the Aiguille d'Argentière. Cross a scree (or snow) slope to get to the lower left bank moraine of the glacier. Go up the crest of the moraine to the foot of the face. 30 mins.

Central Corner is easily recognisable via two patches of light-coloured rock to the left of the third pitch.

START

Climb up leftwards on to a grassy ledge at the foot of a rightward-slanting and quickly steepening crack.

The magnificent corner of pitch 5.

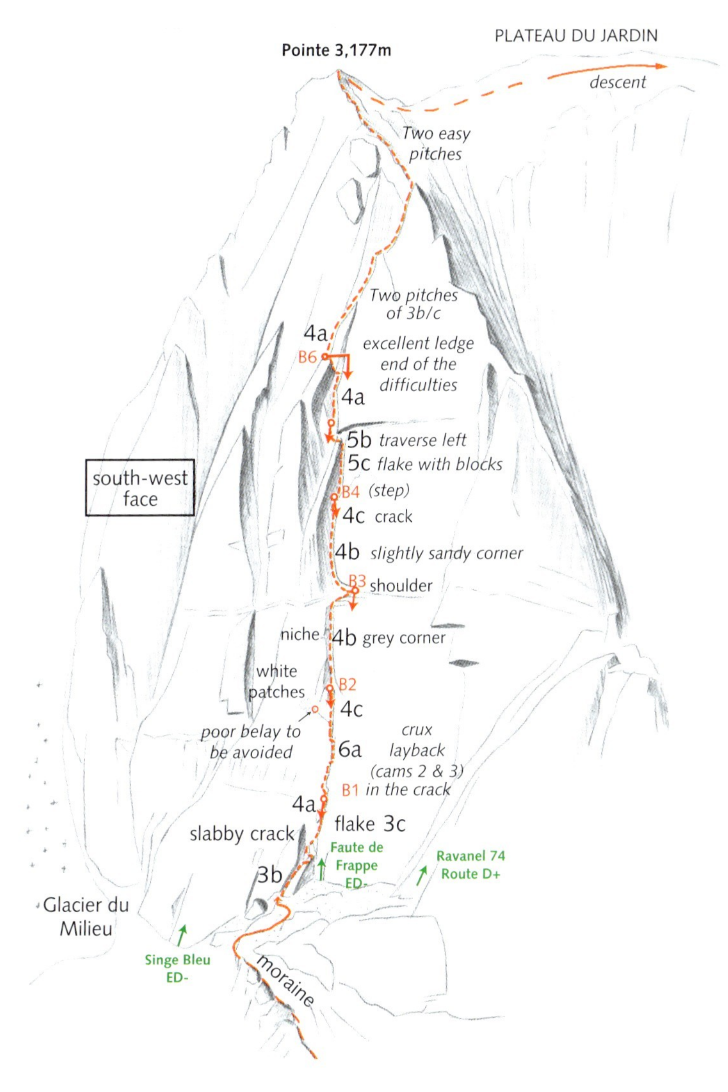

DESCENT

(a) Either abseil from B6.

(b) Or continue to the summit: climb five more pitches (4a then 3c), first diagonally rightwards, then move back left on to the ridgeline (3,177m). **NB:** usually there are no abseil stations in this section. Head diagonally rightwards across the gently sloping terrace of the Plateau (large boulders and slabs). Just before the top of the Plateau, move across to gain its eastern edge at the top of an open, striated chimney on the Améthystes face. Go down the chimney for about 40m, traverse right across large pink slabs, then move back below the chimney to a small notch. Head east down the gully to the right bank moraine of the Glacier des Améthystes. Easy ground (south-west) leads back to the hut. 1½ hrs from the summit.

AIGUILLE DU REFUGE (3,057M)

SOUTH FACE: GÂTEAU DE RIZ

START POINT: Argentière Hut (2,771m), 1½ hrs from top of the Grands Montets cable car. See pages 94–95.
DIFFICULTY: D, 4c oblig. Homogenous series of pitches if you follow the original line. Varied and airy climbing. Nuts and cams to supplement old and widely spaced *in situ* gear (pegs). Complex route finding.
TIMES: approach 10 mins; route 3 hrs; descent 35 mins.
VERTICAL HEIGHT: 200m.
CONDITIONS: dries quickly.
GEAR: two sets of cams 2.5–3, plus small nuts for the variants.
FIRST ASCENT: M. Piola, A. Muller & B. Wietliesbach, 27 December 1975.

The aptly named Aiguille du Refuge seems to be rooted in the foundations of the hut at its foot. Sitting on the terrace, drink in hand, you can watch the antics of the climbers above, as long as you don't mind getting a crick in your neck! You will quickly see that *Gâteau de Riz* reserves several surprises – aficionados particularly look out for the moment climbers straddle the famous 'Lucky Luke' crack before scaling the golden granite of the summit pitches.

Now it is time for you to have a go. It's a ten-minute approach. Can you cope?

APPROACH

Head north up the grassy slopes above the hut. The route starts to the left of a reddish spur on the left side of the south face.

DESCENT

Abseil (25m) down the north-west face to a steep gully on the west face. Do not abseil down this gully (slings visible), but traverse north-west below the overhangs, going up slightly to reach an obvious ridge below the summit spires (70m, 3a) and a wide, rocky gully. Go down this gully (west), then head south-east back to the hut. 40 mins.

The rock is always fabulous, such as here on P4.

5

Aiguille du Refuge
3,057m
move on to a ledge on north-west face, then 25m abseil
70m traverse 3a
descent gully
4a
4c
5b
B7
4a
3b
B6
exposed crest
notch
3b
B5
orange gendarme
4c
chimney
4a
B4
south face
4a
5c
4c cracked slab
B3
Lucky Luke crack straddle then move onto slab
sentry box
4c
easy ridge
B2
4a
4b
B1
chimney
4c
crack
Gâteau de Riz

AIGUILLE DU GÉNÉPI (3,059M)

SOUTH FACE: GÉNÉPI RIDGE & MORT DE RIRE

START POINT: Argentière Hut (2,771m), 1½ hrs from the top of the Grands Montets cable car. See pages 94–95.
TIMES: approach 20 mins; route 3 hrs; descent 25 mins.
VERTICAL HEIGHTS: *Génépi Ridge*, 200m; *Mort de Rire*, 250m.
CONDITIONS: modest altitude, steep rock and south facing, what more could you want?
GEAR: mid-size nuts and cams.
FIRST ASCENTS: *Génépi Ridge*: H. Biondi, P. Darlot & R. Ravanel, 7 September 1977; *Mort de Rire*: F. Burnier with a UCPA group, August 1988.

The Aiguille du Génépi looks across the Glacier des Améthystes towards the proud and solitary summits of the Dolent and the Triolet. Compared with these mighty peaks, its south face appears very small, not much bigger than many valley crags.

The *Génépi Ridge* is ideal as a first mountain route, combining increasingly airy climbing on outstanding rock with an entertaining finish. *Mort de Rire* is a more challenging proposition, involving six fantastic pitches on superbly featured rock and a finale that will sharpen your route finding skills.

APPROACH

Follow the water pipe from the hut (north-east). Do not head straight to the moraine; instead, go left up the boulder field to the foot of the face (to the east of the Aiguille du Refuge). 20 mins.

GÉNÉPI RIDGE

D, 5b oblig. Aesthetic and varied. Quite sustained crack climbing on pitches 1 and 2. The last two pitches are more intimidating than difficult. Widely spaced *in situ* gear. Some belays need backing up.

The thin crack on pitch 2 (5a) of the *Génépi Ridge*.

DESCENT

Abseil (25m) down the north face to a notch. Go down stepped ledges on the Améthystes side to get back to the foot of the face. 25 mins. It is possible to escape from B6 by doing two abseils on the east face, then descending stepped ledges.

MORT DE RIRE

D+, 200m, 5c oblig, one move of 6a or A0 (peg in the overhang). Widely spaced bolts plus easy-to-place cams and nuts. Complex route finding on the upper section.

START

At an obvious flake (one bolt), 20m to the right of the large roof at the foot of the wall.

DESCENT

Abseil down the route from B6, or do two 45m abseils on the east face and then descend stepped ledges, or finish up the *Génépi Ridge*.

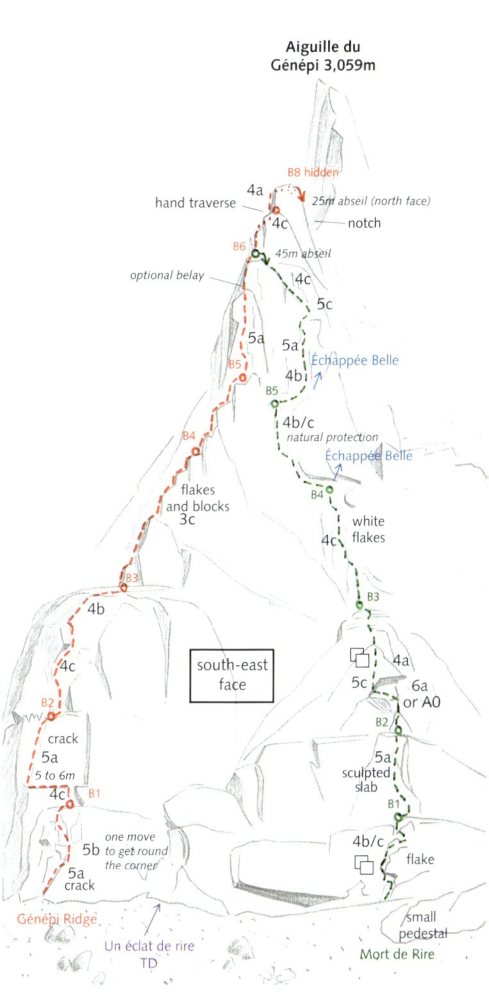

Starting the crux pitch (P3) of *Mort de Rire*.

The Aiguille du Génépi, to the right of the Aiguille du Refuge.

POINTE DE BAYÈRE (2,700M)

SOUTH-WEST SPUR: RAVANEL ROUTE

START POINT: Argentière, cable car to the top of the Grands Montets (3,295m). See page 95.
DIFFICULTY: D, 5b oblig. Classic granite corner climbing. Some *in situ* gear plus nuts and cams. Complex route finding in the upper section. Glacier approach and steep descent.
TIMES: approach 45 mins; route 2–3 hrs; descent 45 mins to get back to the Lognan cable car station.
VERTICAL HEIGHT: 200m.
CONDITIONS: sunny aspect, dries quickly.
GEAR: crampons, ice axe, two long slings for the large blocks at the belays, nuts, cams 1–3.
FIRST ASCENT: A. Comte, J.-M. Roche & R. Ravanel, 23 June 1976.

With its views of the Drus and the Nant Blanc, sunny aspect and easy access from the cable car, Pointe de Bayère is a choice objective. The route's seven pitches follow a series of classic corners on wonderfully rough granite and the quality of the climbing more than compensates for having to carry glacier gear on the route, especially if you do the slightly more difficult variant.

APPROACH

Go down the steps from the cable car station to the Glacier des Grands Montets. Descend the glacier westwards to its tongue. Continue down the steep slopes below the glacier, bearing right to follow the foot of the cliffs. At the bottom of the snowy combe, follow a series of ledges to a boulder field, just before a steep break of slope. 45 mins.

Start on the right side of the spur. Climb leftward-slanting ledges to a platform (pegs) at the foot of a slightly grassy corner.

DESCENT

On the north face. From B6, head right for 120m to a shoulder (2,700m). Go down north-facing slopes to just before the top of the Bochard gondola lift. Follow the valley on the right, first going down the Glacier de la Pendant and then following the ski slopes to the midway cable car station at Lognan (1,973m). 45 mins.

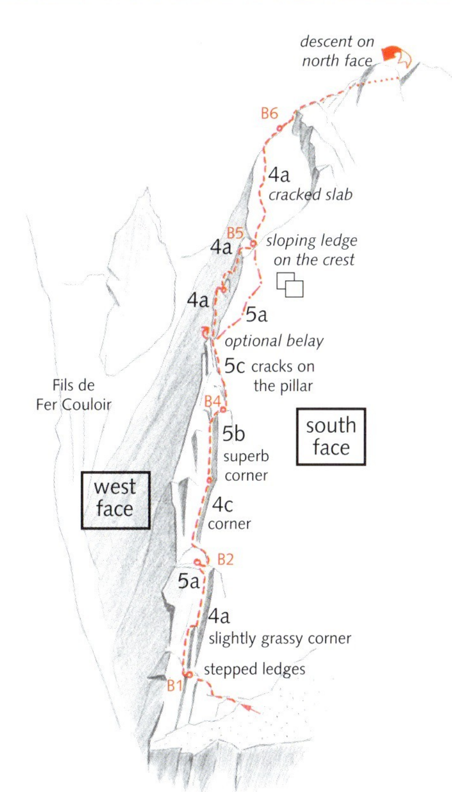

Above: The spur, showing the approach from the Grands Montets.

Below: Looking across the summit slab to the Aiguille Verte.

Opposite: Corners and perfect rock epitomise the route, such as here on P2 (5a).

LOWER SLABS OF THE ENVERS

EAST FACE: 20,000 LIEUES SOUS LA NEIGE, GEORGES, PILIER DES RHODO-DINDONS

START POINT: Chamonix, then train to Montenvers station (1,913m). See page 95.
TIMES: approach 1½ hrs; routes 3 hrs; abseils 1½ hrs; descent to Montenvers 1¼ hrs.
VERTICAL HEIGHT: 280m.
CONDITIONS: seepage lines early in the season and after rain.
GEAR: ice axe/crampons (Mer de Glace can be slippery), two sets of medium nuts, cams 0.5–3.
FIRST ASCENTS: *20,000 Lieues*: R. Ghilini & M. Piola, 26 September 1983 (rebolted in 2002); *Georges*: G. Bettembourg, R. Ghilini & M. Piola, 8 July 1983 (rebolted in 2005); *Rhodo-dindons*: G. Hopfgartner, M. Piola & P.-A. Steiner, 12 July 1984 (rebolted in 2001).

The extraordinary slabs below the Envers Hut, in the glorious setting of the Mer de Glace, have long attracted climbers. At first acquaintance, these smooth granite walls, patiently scoured and polished by the river of ice, can be perplexing to climb on – with even the stickiest of rock shoes you can find your feet skittering across the rock!

At the Envers, climbers of all levels can find routes suited to their abilities: The *Pilier des Rhodo-dindons* is ideal for learning to smear; *Georges* combines friction climbing with the need to place nuts and cams; and the superbly varied *20,000 Lieues* includes an almost perfect crack.

APPROACH

Head south along the path from Montenvers station and go down the ladders to the Mer de Glace. Go up the glacier, trending left to reach its centre at around 2,000m. Stay to the right of Les Moulins (area of glacial mills), bearing south to reach the left bank of the glacier at around 2,150m. The slabs lie between two streams below spot height 2,406m on the IGN map. 1½ hrs.

DESCENT

Abseil down the route, then retrace your steps back to Montenvers.

20,000 LIEUES SOUS LA NEIGE

TD-, 6a oblig. Technical crack climbing on P4: 40m with a 6a move at the start, after which there is no more *in situ* gear but protection is easy to place and there are several resting places. The upper section is very pure. Take two or three extra medium-sized cams.

Notes: P1 climbs a smooth, steep wall (6b, Fixe glue-in bolts) that can be avoided by starting up the *Pilier des Rhodo-dindons* and then traversing left, either level with the first belay or from the middle of P2. B2 is at the start of the ledge. Traverse along this ledge for 50m to B3 at the foot of the crack.

GEORGES

TD-, 6a oblig. Varied and delicate climbing. Sustained lower section. Little *in situ* gear but easy to protect.

Continued …

8

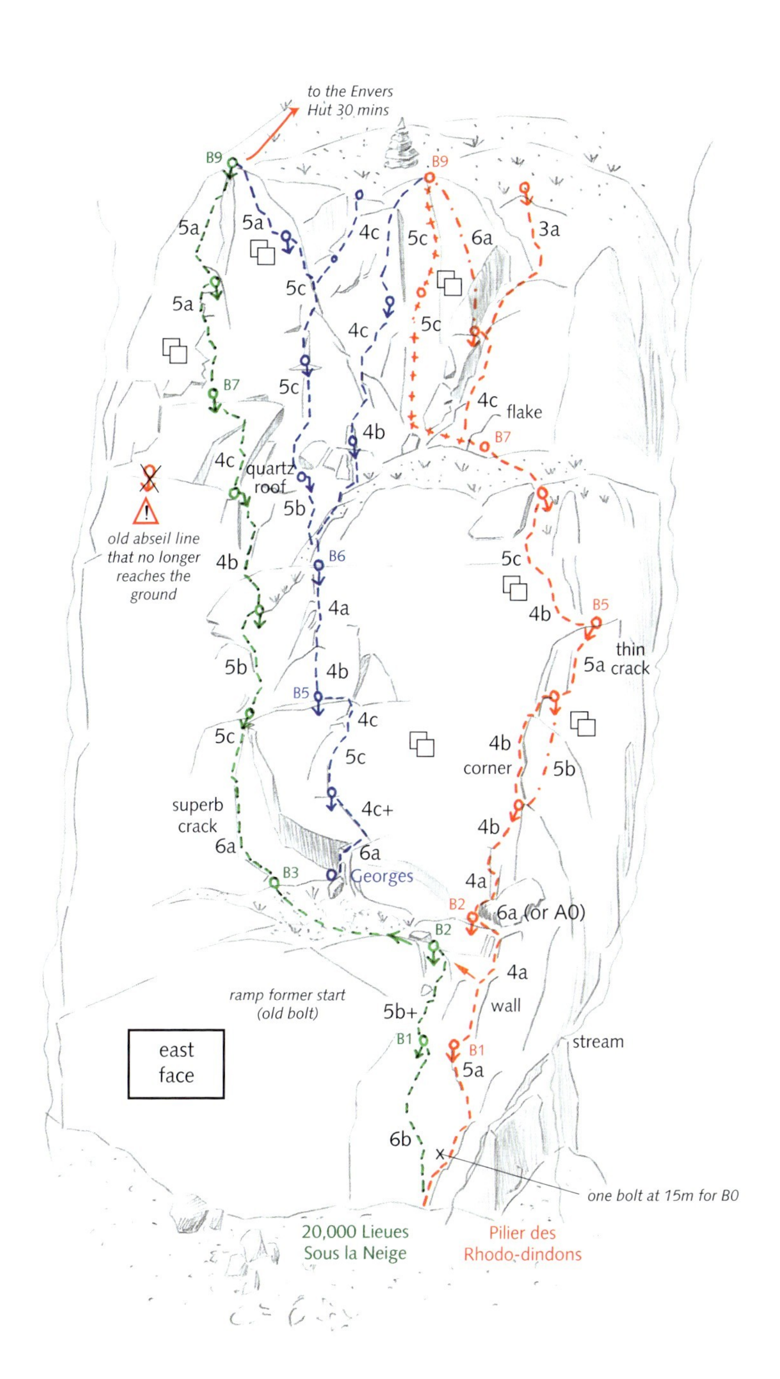
to the Envers Hut 30 mins
B9
5a
5a
4c
5c
6a
3a
5a
5c
5c
4c
5c
B7
5c
4c
flake
4b
B7
4c
quartz roof
5b
old abseil line that no longer reaches the ground
4b
B6
5c
4a
4b
B5
5b
4b
B5
5a
thin crack
4c
5c
5c
4b
corner
5b
superb crack
4c+
4b
6a
6a
B3
Georges
4a
B2
6a (or A0)
B2
4a
ramp former start (old bolt)
5b+
wall
B1
B1
stream
5a
east face
6b
x
one bolt at 15m for B0
20,000 Lieues Sous la Neige
Pilier des Rhodo-dindons

LOWER SLABS OF THE ENVERS

EAST FACE: 20,000 LIEUES SOUS LA NEIGE, GEORGES, PILIER DES RHODO-DINDONS

Notes: The collapse of the moraine has altered the start. To avoid increasing the difficulty, start up the *Pilier des Rhodo-dindons*, then traverse left in the middle of P2 to B2 of *20,000 Lieues*, at the start of the ledge. From here, traverse to B3 on a block to the right of the big roof. From B6, do not go left (slab, three bolts, junction with *20,000 Lieues*).

Two possible finishes:

(a) The original finish (4c), on the right.

(b) A new finish climbed in 2005 (5c), on the left.

PILIER DES RHODO-DINDONS

D+, 5c oblig, one move of 6a (or A0). The easiest route but in the same style. Good for practising placing natural protection. Two sections of delicate slab climbing, the rest follows cracks.

START

The route starts up an easy slanting ramp parallel to the waterfall and then climbs a crack on the left. P1 is longer than 50m but it is possible to take an intermediate belay on a single bolt (backed up with a small nut) 15m above the ground.

Above: The confluence of the Mer de Glace and the Glacier de Leschaux.

Opposite: The unforgettable crack on *20,000 Lieues*.

P1 of *Rhodo-dindons*.

8

AIGUILLE DE BLAITIÈRE: FIRST AND SECOND TOWERS OF THE SOUTH-EAST RIDGE

SOUTH FACE: MAGIE D'ORIENT, L'OPIUM DU PEUPLE

START POINT: Envers des Aiguilles Hut (2,523m), 2½ hrs from Montenvers station. See pages 94–95.
TIMES: approach 45 mins; routes 3–4 hrs; abseils 1–2 hrs.
VERTICAL HEIGHTS: 250 to 300m.
CONDITIONS: steep and sunny therefore quickly in condition, but be wary of snow on the ledges, which can lead to wet streaks. Dries quickly after rain.
GEAR: ice axe and crampons for the approach, 12 quickdraws, nuts, cams 0.5–3.5.
FIRST ASCENTS: *Magie d'Orient*: M. Motto & M. Piola, 4 September 1994; *Opium*: V. Sprüngli & M. Piola, 6 August 1996.

The Envers des Aiguilles bears the hallmark of a truly outstanding climber, Michel Piola. The area was his favourite playground in the early 1980s, when the bolting of routes first took off. By placing bolts to complement natural protection, he opened up a world of otherwise unprotectable rock to middle-grade climbers. What followed is part of climbing history – an impressive number of magnificent routes throughout the area, including the Aiguilles Rouges. For this, he deserves our warmest thanks.

Magie d'Orient, enchanting and pristine, is the easiest line here, although the descent includes a tricky abseil from the second tower.

MAGIE D'ORIENT

TD-, 6a oblig. Varied climbing, slabs and cracks. After a thuggy start, the route takes the easiest line to B3, from where it follows a logical line at a consistent standard up the first tower. P5 is a superb layback crack with jams for placing gear.

The descent involves a diagonal abseil across the snowfield between the two towers.

It could be Arabia, but where are the genies?

The 5c layback on P5 of *Magie d'Orient*.

Notes: Stay on the right-hand line of cracks on the second tower.

L'OPIUM DU PEUPLE

TD, 6a oblig. Similar to *Magie d'Orient* but more sustained.

The route the furthest right on the first tower: start up a nice slab (sustained 5c), 7m to the right of *Magie d'Orient,* which it crosses on P3. On the second tower, it is the line to the left of *Magie,* whose final pitch it shares.

APPROACH

From the hut, contour round southwards below the northern branch of the Glacier d'Envers de Blaitière. Go up the southern branch of the glacier (crevasses, often bare ice), heading south-west to the foot of the face. 35 mins.

DESCENT

If you stop after the first tower, abseil down *Opium.* If you continue to the top of the second tower, do three abseils to get to B7bis on *Magie d'Orient,* then abseil (35m) down the chimney below to a belay 3m above the snowfield. Abseil diagonally rightwards, then go back up the snowfield to the edge of the first tower. The next abseil leads to B3, on the wide ledge.

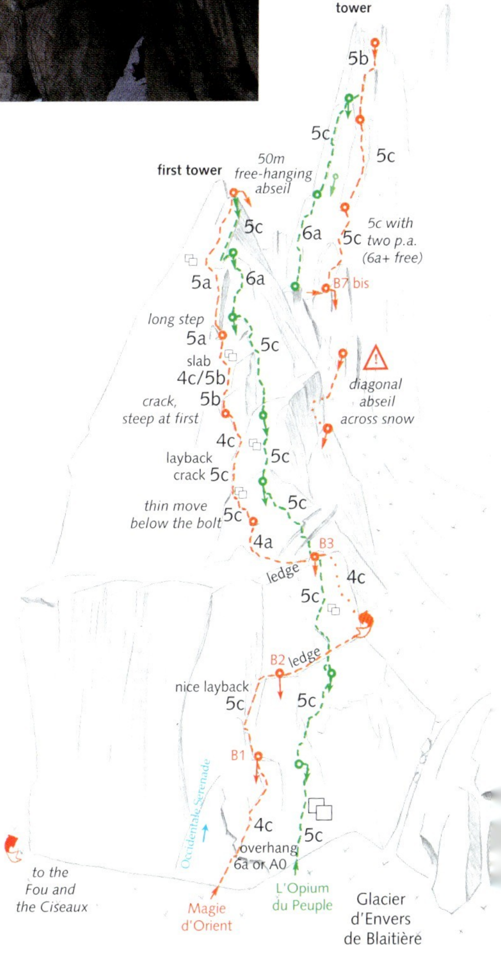

PREMIÈRE POINTE DES NANTILLONS (2,921M)

SOUTH-EAST FACE: AMAZONIA, BIENVENUE AU GEORGES V

START POINT: Envers des Aiguilles Hut (2,523m), 2½ hrs from Montenvers station. See page 94.
TIMES: approach 20 mins; routes 4–5 hrs; abseils 2 hrs.
VERTICAL HEIGHT: 370m.
CONDITIONS: the upper section tends to stay wet the longest.
GEAR: ice axe/crampons for the approach, 12 quickdraws, two sets of medium nuts, cams 0.5–3.5.
FIRST ASCENTS: *Amazonia*: G. Hopfgartner & M. Piola, 2 September 1984 (rebolted in 2003 with modifications to P5 and P6); *Bienvenue au Georges V*: M. Piola & P. Strappazzon, 3/4 September 1986 (rebolted in 2004).

Most of the routes at the Envers have bolt belays but the only fixed runners are in areas without cracks for nuts or cams. As a result, climbers must be able to place natural protection on pitches that can be quite strenuous.

Bienvenue au Georges V is *the* great classic of the Envers. It climbs a series of good, honest cracks linked by sections of quite bold slab climbing. In contrast, *Amazonia* is more technical and remarkably sustained. You feel very small when you are sitting on top of the very sharp and airy summit.

APPROACH

From the hut, contour round southwards below the northern branch of the Glacier d'Envers de Blaitière. The face is above, on the right. 20 mins.

AMAZONIA

TD+, 6a oblig. (climbers should be capable of climbing 6a+ for P1). Few easy pitches. Corners and cracks, except the slab on P1. The first half is the most sustained.

Notes: B0 is on a flake – its height above the glacier depends on snow cover. P1 is a bold, slabby traverse followed by a thin crack up a steep slab (requires micro-nuts and cams, including two Friend 2.5 size). Pitches above B8 are shared with *Guy-Anne*.

Variant between B3 and B6 on the pillar on the right, 6a+ (first climbed in 2003).

DESCENT

The belays are equipped for abseiling but it is better to use the independent abseil line between *Amazonia* and *Bienvenue*.

If you abseil the route, a 50m abseil from B3 leads to a wide ledge above B1 (chain and maillon).

The delicate first pitch of *Amazonia* (6a+).

BIENVENUE AU GEORGES V

TD+, 6a oblig. Easy to protect cracks and sparsely bolted slabs but with incut holds.

Notes: Start up a steep crack (*L'Age d'Homme* heads off left below the overhang, grey Fixe bolt hangers) then head right across a delicate, smooth slab (6a+, Petzl bolts).

P5: above the belay, move 5m left to climb an unpleasant looking crack (overhanging, 5a).

P7 to P9: crux pitches, spaced bolts on P9 (6a).

DESCENT

Abseil down the route or down the abseil line between *Bienvenue* and *Amazonia*.

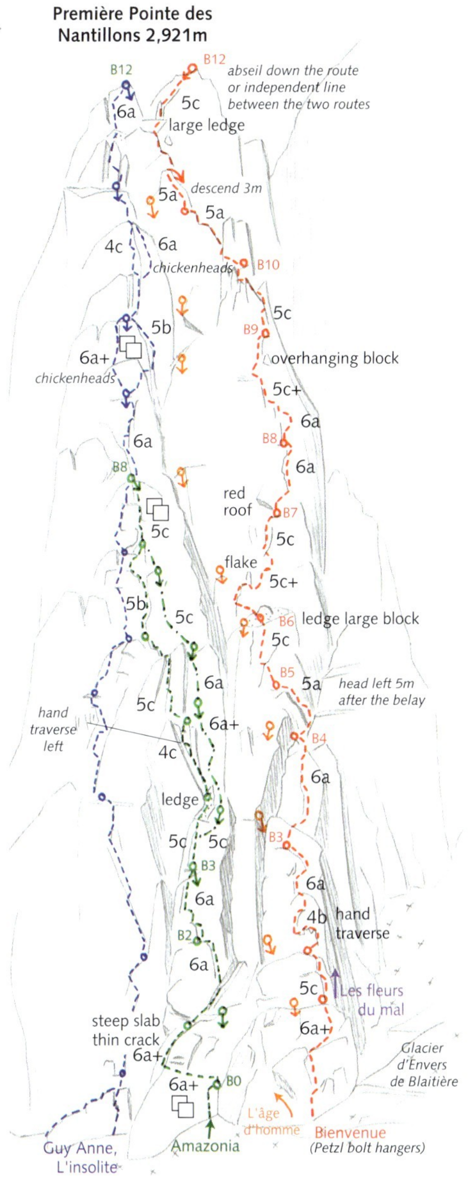

TOUR ROUGE (2,899M)

EAST FACE: MARCHAND DE SABLE

START POINT: Envers des Aiguilles Hut (2,523m), 2½ hrs from Montenvers station. See page 95.
DIFFICULTY: TD+, 6a oblig. (climbers should be capable of climbing 6a+). Very sustained and demanding. Little *in situ* protection. Bold climbing between runners with few rests on the crux sections. Notably the case on P5 and P6 and especially on P9, where there is potential for a huge fall.
TIMES: approach 30 mins; climb 3–4 hrs; abseils 2 hrs.
VERTICAL HEIGHT: 300m.
CONDITIONS: steep and sunny, dries quite quickly.
GEAR: ice axe/crampons for the approach, 12 quickdraws, two sets of small and medium nuts, cams 0.5–3.5, doubling up on medium sizes.
FIRST ASCENT: G. Hopfgartner & M. Piola, 19/20 July 1983. Rebolted in 1996, and then in 2003 for the starting slab.

Marchand de Sable **is horrendously bold – a mixture of cams, conviction and painful jams. It is often said to be one of the best routes in the massif, a truly classy climb.**

APPROACH

Head west from the hut. Go up a muddy gully to a small notch at the foot of the spur of the Tour Verte. Climb easy cracks on the left to a shoulder 30m above the notch. Follow a ledge rightwards, then traverse across a steep gully to get to the Glacier de Trélaporte. Go up the slope (north-west) to the foot of the face. 30 mins.

START

At the lowest point of the face. Climb a slab to a flake-corner.

DESCENT

Abseil down the route.

The south side of the Chamonix Aiguilles. L–R: *Magie, Amazonia, Bienvenue* and *Marchand de Sable*.

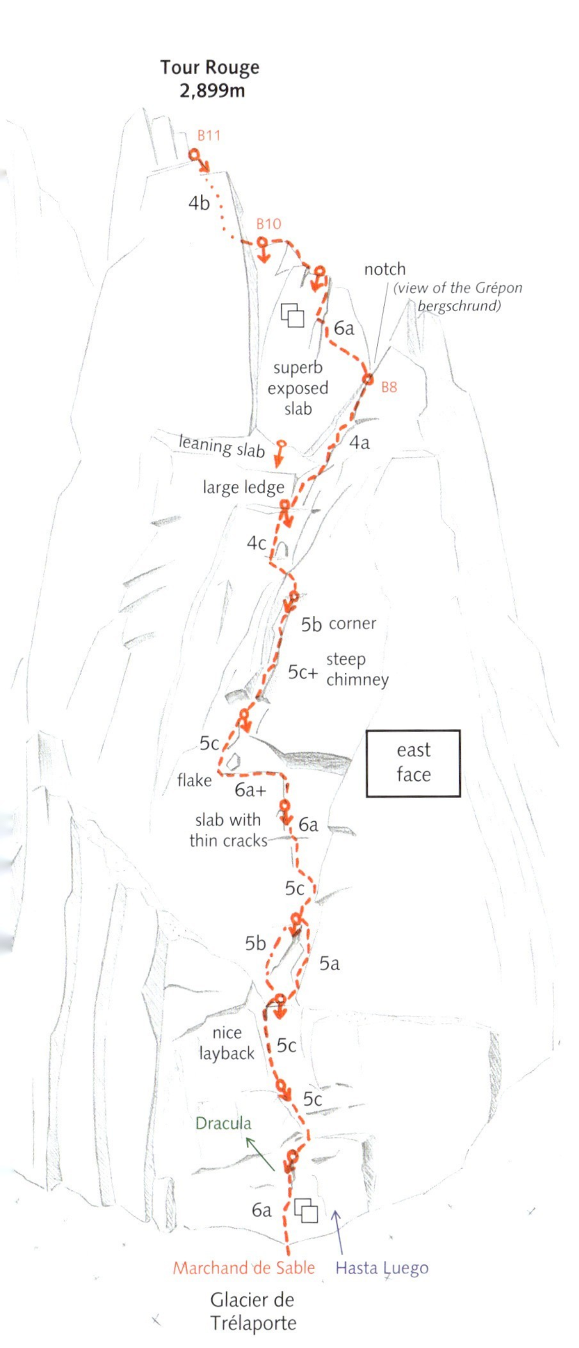

The superb layback on P3 (5c).

The thin crack on P5 (6a).

RED PILLAR OF THE BLAITIÈRE (3,050M)

WEST FACE: NABOT-LÉON

START POINT: Plan de l'Aiguille (2,310m), midway station of the Aiguille du Midi cable car. See page 95.
DIFFICULTY: TD, 5c oblig. Several difficult pitches with sustained climbing. Mostly cracks with little *in situ* protection. Abseil descent from *in situ* belays. Approach includes a 40° snow or ice slope.
TIMES: approach 1½ hrs; climb 2–3 hrs; abseils 1 hr.
VERTICAL HEIGHT: 200m.
CONDITIONS: west-facing, so no need for an early start – the rock can be cold in the morning.
GEAR: crampons and ice axe, ice screws (the approach goes up an ice slope), nuts, cams 0.5–3.
FIRST ASCENT: T. Cerdan & M. Piola, 18 September 1985, rebolted in 1996.

At the foot of the huge west face of the Blaitière you will find a little paradise of perfect rock. The Red Pillar boasts an exceptional concentration of short but quite difficult climbs that require a range of climbing skills – from jamming to laybacking and bridging – and the ability to read the rock. More than a crag, not quite a big wall, it is a place for applying skills, not learning them.

***Nabot-Léon* is the easiest route on the pillar, with sustained pitches on impeccably solid, coarse-grained, multi-coloured granite.**

APPROACH

From the Plan de l'Aiguille, follow the path eastwards below Lac Bleu. Head diagonally upwards past the foot of the Glacier de Blaitière to the right-bank moraine (2,475m). Go past some huge boulders, heading north-east slightly. After a short distance, turn right (south-east) and go up gravelly slopes to the edge of a large hollow dotted with boulders. Cross the hollow, swinging round rightwards to get to the steep snowfield at the foot of the north-west flank of the Aiguille de Blaitière. Go up the right bank of this slope (40°, sometimes ice), then traverse across it and climb a wall of loose rock to a small notch to the south-east of the Lames Fontaine. This leads to the access ledge at the foot of the Red Pillar. 1½ hrs.

DESCENT

Abseil down the route or down *Bobokassa*, on the west-north-west face (seven abseils).

Total harmony on P4 (5a).

The pillar and the approach.

PLAN DE L'AIGUILLE

The steep and technical first pitch (5b).

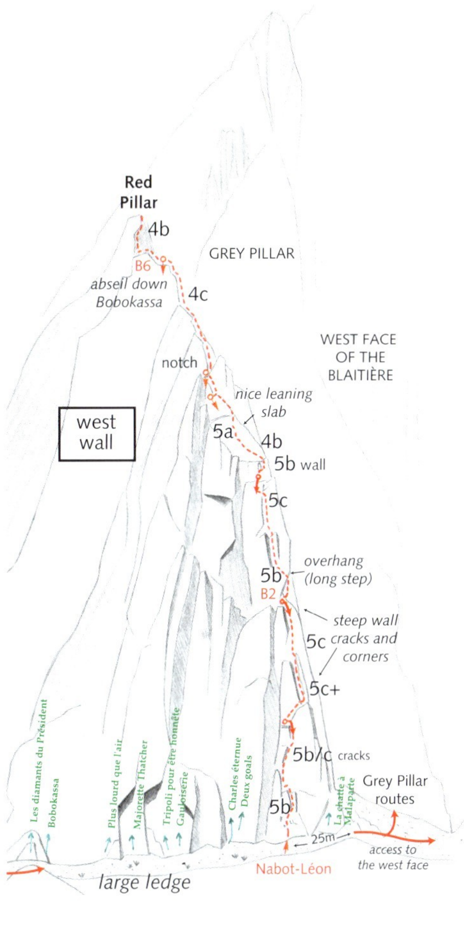

Plan de l'Aiguille, a beach café at altitude.

AIGUILLE DU PEIGNE (3,192M)

LES LÉPIDOPTÈRES & THE NORMAL ROUTE, PAPILLONS RIDGE

START POINT: Plan de l'Aiguille (2,310m), midway station of the Aiguille du Midi cable car. See page 95.

As the archetypal Chamonix-granite rock route, the *Papillons Ridge* used to be swarming with climbers, making any ascent a laborious affair. Now, with the addition of so many new routes, it is possible to savour in peace and quiet this cocktail of athletic free climbing on perfect rock and in fabulously exposed positions.

Les Lépidoptères – a continuous crack up a shield of smooth slabs – can be enough in itself. But, for those who shun the abseil descent, it is also a great way of starting the *Normal Route* to the summit, which threads an astute line up the complex ridge above. Although it avoids all the more difficult steps by traversing along ledges, terraces, chimneys and sharp ridges, you will have to keep an eye on the time if you want to make it down in time to catch the last cable car to Chamonix.

LES LÉPIDOPTERES & THE NORMAL ROUTE

DIFFICULTY: *Les Lépidoptères*: D, 5a oblig. Predominantly cracks and smearing.
Mostly natural protection.
Normal Route to the summit of the Peigne: AD, 4c oblig. Exposed. Complex route finding. Long.
TIMES: approach 1½ hrs; *Les Lépidoptères* 2 hrs; from the notch at 2,800m to the Peigne 2–3 hrs; descent 3–4 hrs.
VERTICAL HEIGHT: *Les Lépidoptères* 200m, + around 400m for the summit.
CONDITIONS: generally July to September, once the snow has melted. *Les Lépidoptères* faces north-west and the upper part of the Peigne includes sections on the north face. In the shade in the morning. Dangerous in stormy weather.
GEAR: ice axe and crampons depending on the state of the snowfield on the approach.
Long slings, nuts, cams 1–3.
FIRST ASCENTS: *Les Lépidoptères*: M. Armand & M. Piola, 28 July 1986.
The Peigne: G. Liégeard & R. O'Gorman, with J. Ravanel & J. Couttet, 23 July 1906.

A perfect crack on the third tower of the Papillons.

APPROACH

From the Plan de l'Aiguille (2,310m), head south-east past the café and follow a faint path up grassy slopes towards the foot of the *Papillons Ridge*, marked by some huge, green-ish blocks. At around 2,400m, bear left towards an obvious rock pillar at the foot of the north-west face. Head diagonally across a scree slope and go round the top of this pillar to the foot of the face. Traverse below the face (steep snow late into the season) for about 100m to the foot of a wall split by a crack. Climb this crack (20m, 4b), then head east for about 80m before heading back diagonally west to go up a ledge system to the foot of the route (to the right of the smooth slabs). Large ledge, one bolt + slings. 1½ hrs from the Plan.

PLAN DE L'AIGUILLE

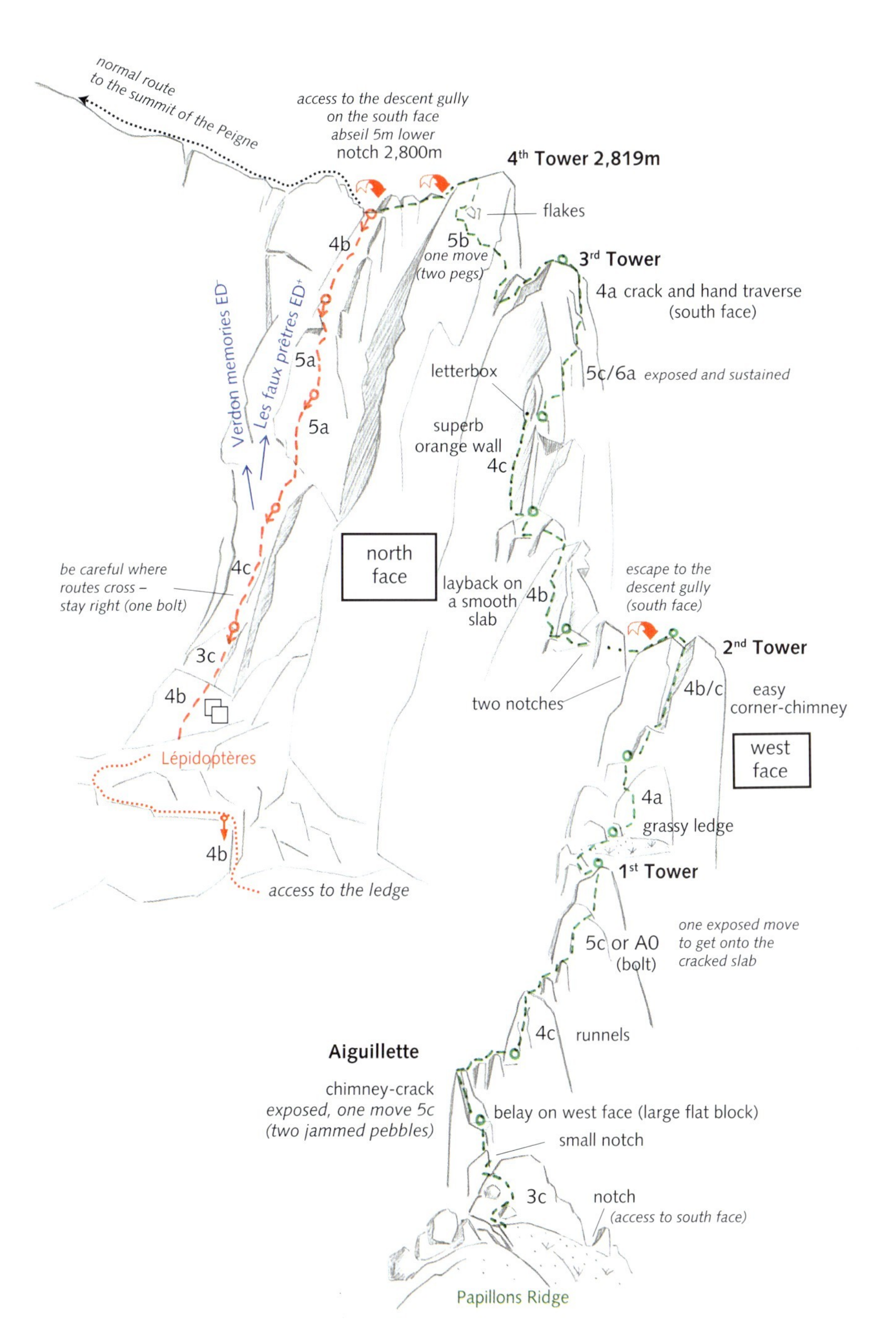

AIGUILLE DU PEIGNE

LES LÉPIDOPTÈRES & THE NORMAL ROUTE, PAPILLONS RIDGE

LES LÉPIDOPTÈRES

Head diagonally rightwards across the slab, then climb a thin crack and vague corner. B1 on a good ledge. Continue up cracks for four pitches to the notch at 2,800m (one bolt + maillon at each belay).

DESCENT

Abseil down the route, or descend the Papillons couloir (gained by a 50m abseil on the south face, just below the notch).

NORMAL ROUTE

From the notch, follow the almost horizontal ridge leftwards (3/4b) to a wide ledge that runs eastwards above the lower slabs on the Chamonix face. Follow this ledge leftwards for about 100m, then head rightwards up cracked slabs for about 80m (quartz veins) to a shallow notch at the foot of the gendarme at 3,009m. Go right round the gendarme by following a chimney-gully for about 60m.

This leads on to the north face, which is often covered in snow. Follow flaky ledges and a ramp on the right (large boulders) to the notch at 3,043m, above a large, reddish gendarme (top of the *Vaucher Route*, 1 hr from the notch at 2,800m).

Climb a steep pitch on the crest of the west ridge (4b, jammed block) to gain a niche of sandy rock by a rightwards traverse on the south-west face. Follow the west ridge to exit via the Lépiney Crack (5c) on the north side of the summit. Descend slightly, then climb runnels leftwards to below an overhang. Traverse diagonally rightwards (rounded slab, then block to climb to get to the 'quartz ledge' – 3/4b, cable, pegs). From here, follow diagonal corners and cracks to the south-east ridge (4c, exposed, flake, two pegs). Follow the narrow ridge (4b) past a notch with a hand-line to gain the summit (2 hrs).

3 hrs from the top of *Les Lépidoptères*.

DESCENT

Go back down the same route to the end of the ledge above the lower slabs. Do two abseils (40m and 30m) down the upper part of the Papillons couloir on the south-west face. Continue down the couloir, first on the left bank, for about 200m to get to an obvious path (cairn) that leads leftwards to the Peigne snowfield. From here, follow the right-bank moraine to the Plan de l'Aiguille. 3–4 hrs from the summit.

PAPILLONS RIDGE

DIFFICULTY: D, 5c oblig. Varied ridge climb. Very airy and exposed. Complex route finding. Few *in situ* belays. Some *in situ* protection on the hardest sections

TIMES: approach 1 hr; climb 3 hrs; descent 1½ hrs from the cable car.

VERTICAL HEIGHT: 250m.

CONDITIONS: July to September. Exposed to bad weather coming in from the west.

GEAR: nuts, cams 1–3.

FIRST ASCENT: H. Cameré & R. Dewas, 12 July 1926.

APPROACH

Follow the first part of the approach to *Les Lépidoptères* but instead of heading left across the scree slope at around 2,400m, continue straight up (south-east) the slope to the top of a grassy pyramid capped by huge green boulders. 1 hr.

START

Start on the north face by climbing an easy wall directly above the approach path.

DESCENT

Via the Papillons couloir, reached by a 50m abseil after the fourth tower (see opposite).

Peigne *Normal Route* and descent.

On *Les Lépidoptères* (4c).

AIGUILLE DU MIDI (3,800M)

SOUTH FACE: RÉBUFFAT ROUTE

START POINT: top of the Aiguille du Midi cable car (3,795m), Cosmiques Hut (3,613m). See pages 94–95.

DIFFICULTY: TD, 6a oblig. Sustained at 5/5c with occasional 6a moves. Very steep and exposed. Requires placing natural protection. Careful route finding in order to avoid getting on to one of the ten routes that cross the line. Effects of altitude and carrying a sack.

TIMES: approach 20 mins via the glacier, 1 hr if approached by abseil; route 3–5 hrs; return 5 mins.

VERTICAL HEIGHT: 250m.

CONDITIONS: the steepness and sunny aspect of the face means it is often in condition in spring and autumn, but it can be very cold if it is windy or foggy. Keep an eye out for changes in the weather.

GEAR: crampons/ice axe if approached via the glacier, small nuts, cams 0.5–3.5, fleece jacket.

FIRST ASCENT: G. Rébuffat & M. Baquet, 13 July 1956.

How often have we passed below the face on our way to other objectives? How many superlatives have we used to express the effect it has and the courage 'they' showed to defy those smooth slabs, the audacity needed to weave a way between those roofs?

Below the roof at the start of the route (4c).

Now it is our turn to give it a go, and the legend weighs heavily. On the S-crack, our fingernails rasp against the quartz crystals and we bury our toes as far as they will go, trying to spot the remains of the bolt placed by Gaston. There it is, where the face is mirror smooth ... Then we are back at the foot of the abseil, on the platform of the Midi, and a nun asks us if we had started off this morning ... We sit back, content, under the crystal-blue sky.

APPROACH

Descend the exposed and sometimes corniced north-east ridge, then head south-west to the foot of the south face. 20 mins.

The original route started at the lowest point of the face but it has become customary to start via the *Contamine Route*, a pitch higher up and to the right (good ledge with a bolt).

Notes: If you approach by abseil there is a good chance of getting lost if you don't know the face well, and of getting in the way of other climbers. In addition, if you have to retreat for any reason, you will have to descend the glacier in rock shoes without an ice axe or crampons.

The original finish went round the summit tower on to the north face to finish up an often icy crack. The two options described here have become the standard ways of finishing the route.

14

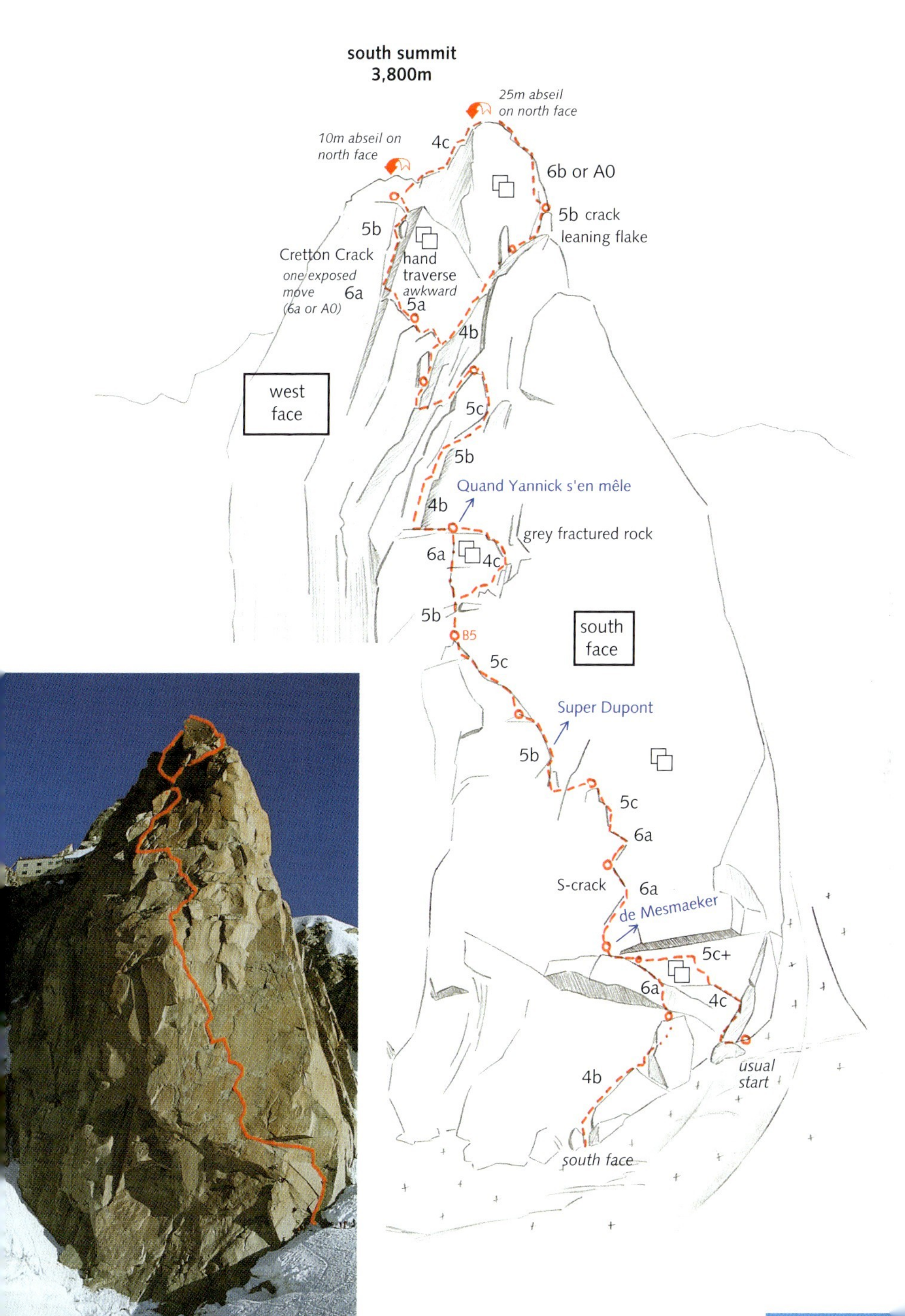
south summit
3,800m
25m abseil on north face
10m abseil on north face
4c
6b or A0
5b crack
leaning flake
5b
Cretton Crack
one exposed move (6a or A0)
6a
hand traverse awkward
5a
4b
west face
5c
5b
Quand Yannick s'en mêle
4b
grey fractured rock
6a
4c
5b
B5
5c
south face
Super Dupont
5b
5c
6a
S-crack
6a
de Mesmaeker
5c+
6a
4c
usual start
4b
south face

PYRAMIDE DU TACUL (3,468M)

EAST RIDGE

START POINT: Pointe Helbronner (3,462m), Torino Hut (3,371m) or Aiguille du Midi (3,795m). See pages 94–95.

DIFFICULTY: AD+, 4c oblig. Mostly grade 4 with one move of 5a. Some natural protection in the lower section. Belays equipped for an abseil descent (be prepared to back up the slings). Glacier approach and bergschrund sometimes difficult to cross.

TIMES: approach 50 mins from the Torino Hut (1 hr from the Aig. du Midi); route 2–3 hrs; abseils 1 hr; return to the Torino Hut 1½ hrs (Aig. du Midi 2 hrs).

VERTICAL HEIGHT: approx. 250m.

CONDITIONS: from May to October. Dries very quickly.

GEAR: crampons, ice axe, ice screws, nuts, cams 2–3.

FIRST ASCENT: E. Croux, L. Grivel & A. Ottoz, 29 July 1940.

The *East Ridge* of the Pyramide, in the heart of the Vallée Blanche, is an excellent introduction to high-mountain rock climbing. Following a logical line, mostly on cracks, and with an abseil descent, the climbing is all about lightness, not least because ice axes and crampons can be left at the foot. In addition, a light touch is needed in places, as the large temperature variations at altitude mean that not all the holds are completely reliable. However, the rock improves as you gain height, turning a beautiful fawn colour below the superb summit spire.

APPROACH

From Pointe Helbronner (the best approach as it facilitates the return), head north-west and pass below the hanging cable car pylon. At the Col des Flambeaux (3,407m), go diagonally leftwards (west) down the steep slope below the Aiguille de Toule to around 3,250m. Traverse north-west between large crevasses to go past the foot of the east ridge of Pointe Adolphe Rey. Trend leftwards and slightly upwards into the glacial basin between Pointe Adolphe Rey and the Pyramide (do not linger below the seracs). Cross the bergschrund below the south flank of the Pyramide, around 50m below the base of the ridge (approx. 3,220m). 50 mins.

DESCENT

Do three abseils down the route to get back to B7, then follow the abseil line down the south-east face (six abseils, max. 50m).

Nearing the top of the ridge (4c).

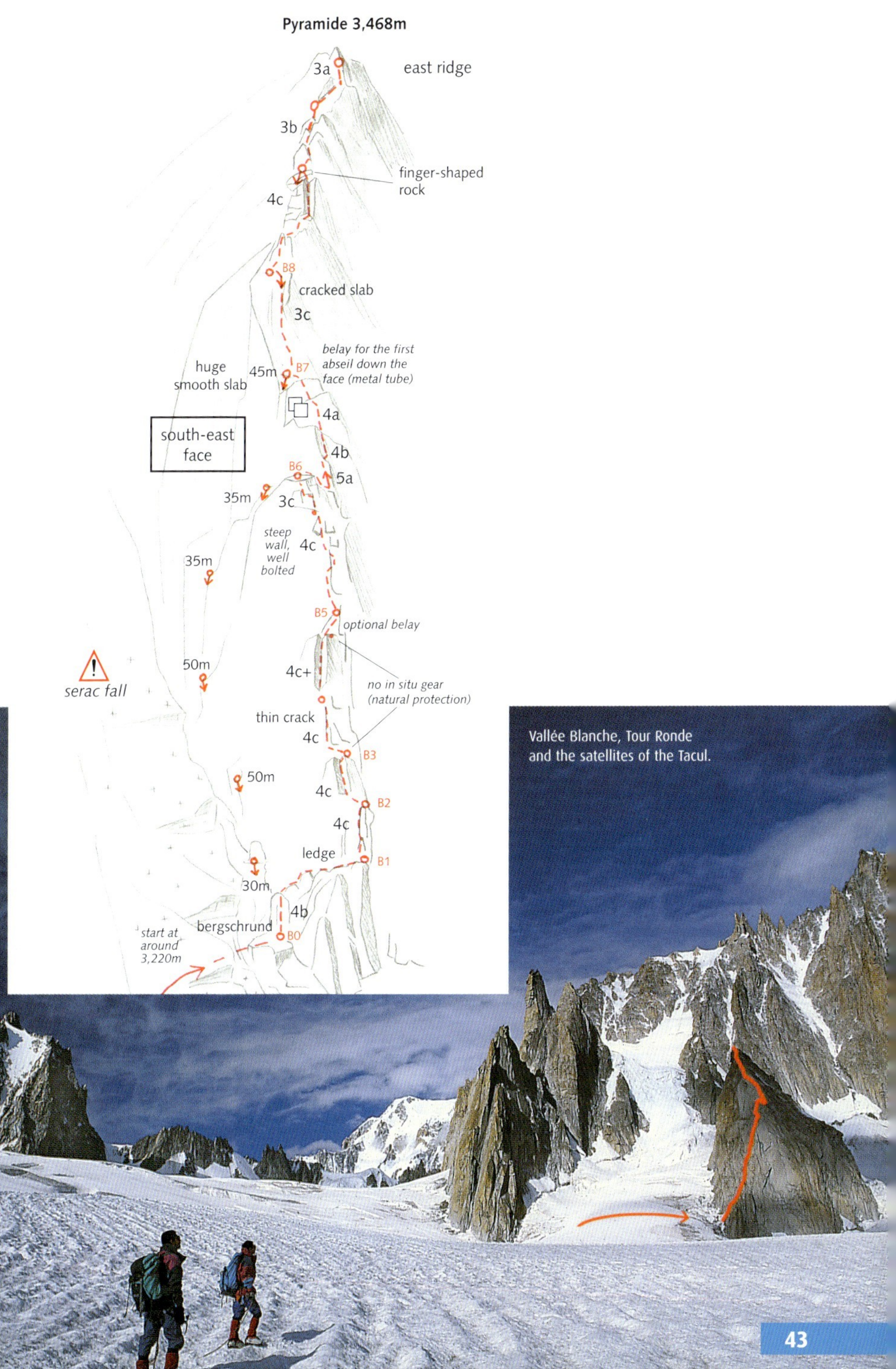

Vallée Blanche, Tour Ronde and the satellites of the Tacul.

POINTE ADOLPHE REY (3,536M)

SOUTH-EAST RIDGE: SALLUARD ROUTE

START POINT: Pointe Helbronner (3,462m), Torino Hut (3,371m) or Aiguille du Midi (3,795m). See pages 94–95.

DIFFICULTY: TD, 6a, 5c oblig. Quite strenuous climbing. Mostly cracks with two steep slab pitches. Requires nuts and cams. Abseil descent down another face. Glacier approach.

TIMES: approach 45 mins; route 4 hrs; abseils 1 hr; return to Helbronner 1½ hrs.

VERTICAL HEIGHT: 300m.

CONDITIONS: usually July to October (a section on the north face can be icy). Best avoided if there is a risk of thunderstorms.

GEAR: crampons, ice axe, ice screws, 12 quickdraws, nuts, cams 1–3.

FIRST ASCENT: T. Busi & F. Salluard, 6 September 1951.

A picture-postcard setting, pure lines, golden granite and an idyllic approach ... what more could you want? How about a sunny aspect, so the face is climbable from the first days of spring, when you can still ski down the Vallée Blanche, until well into the Indian summer, when the crowds are gone?

The picture couldn't be more ideal, but to enjoy it you will have to be fit, have the necessary climbing ability and be skilled at placing cams ...

APPROACH

From Helbronner, head north-west to the Col des Flambeaux (3,407m), then go diagonally leftwards down the steep slope below the Aiguille de Toule. At around 3,250m, traverse north-west between the large crevasses to the base of the ridge at the entrance to the Combe Maudite. 45 mins.

START

The route starts on the left-hand of two parallel spurs separated by a corner-chimney with snow at the bottom. Start up this corner-chimney, then bear left up steep ledges for 35m to get on to the crest of the spur. Belay below an obvious overhang that bars access to the pillar and marks the start of the route.

Note: From B8, descend slightly on the south side, then climb a smooth corner (5c). Hand-traverse left (3c) and climb a short wall that leads to a small notch below the summit. Climb the final wall, then go right round a slab and exit on to the summit (4a).

DESCENT

On the south-west face. Do a 15m abseil to get to the foot of the wall below the summit. A 35m abseil (note the position of the abseil station on the way up) leads to a wide ledge on the south face. Follow this ledge rightwards (looking out) to an abseil station at the top of the huge corner-chimney on the south-west face. Descend this corner-chimney in two 30m abseils (good ledges).

A final 50m abseil takes you over the bergschrund and on to the glacier in the Combe Maudite. 1hr.

From here, go past the north face of the Tour Ronde and back up to the Col des Flambeaux and Helbronner. 1½ hrs. (2½ hrs for the Aiguille du Midi).

Note: From B6 it is possible to climb to the top of the first tower (5b), and then abseil back down the route without going to the true summit. This allows you to leave rucksacks and glacier gear at the foot of the route. In this case, it is worth starting the route by climbing the left flank of the pillar (rightward trending ramp and large ledge on which to gear up).

In the background, the Grand and Petit Capucins.

Opposite page: On the central wall (5a).

LE ROI DE SIAM (3,600M)

SOUTH-EAST FACE: LE LIFTING DU ROI

START POINT: Pointe Helbronner (3,462m) or the Torino Hut (3,371m). Direct cable car access from Italy or reached from France by traversing the Vallée Blanche (2½ hrs or gondola). See pages 94–95.
DIFFICULTY: D+, 5c oblig. Slabs and cracks. *In situ* belays (abseils). A few pegs and bolts in the pitches but nuts and cams needed. Glacier approach
TIMES: approach 1 hr; route 3 hrs; abseils 1¼ hrs; return to Helbronner 1½ hrs.
VERTICAL HEIGHT: 200m
CONDITIONS: climbable from spring to autumn thanks to the sunny aspect and modest altitude. Snow may remain on ledges but should not be too problematical.
GEAR: crampons/ice axe, ice screws, cams 1.5-3, nuts.
FIRST ASCENT: Massimo Datrino & Marco Sperone, summer 2001.

Overshadowed by the Grand and Petit Capucins, which also shelter it from the wind, the Roi de Siam is one of the more discreet granite needles at the foot of Mont Blanc du Tacul. *Le Lifting du Roi* is the best route on its south-east face, giving varied climbing at a consistent standard. It is a route that provides several surprises, all good, such as the steepness of the upper section, especially the last pitch, and the sumptuous, golden granite.

APPROACH

From Helbronner, head north-west to the Col des Flambeaux (3,407m), then bear west and descend to the foot of the Aiguille de Toule at around 3,300m. Continue westwards at more or less this altitude to the Combe Maudite. Once past the north face of the Tour Ronde, head north-west (3,350m contour) until directly below the Roi de Siam, a detached needle in front of the Petit Capucin, and its bergschrund, at around 3,400m. 1 hr.

Notes: During the walk in, look out for the 'two-eared' snowfield at the foot of the face, almost directly below the summit. The route starts just to the left of the left ear. Glacial retreat means the start may be more difficult at the end of the season, but it can be avoided by coming in from the right.

DESCENT

Abseil down the route then follow the approach route back to Helbronner. 1½ hrs.

Granite perfection, just below the summit.

The route, sandwiched between the Grand and the Petit Capucin.

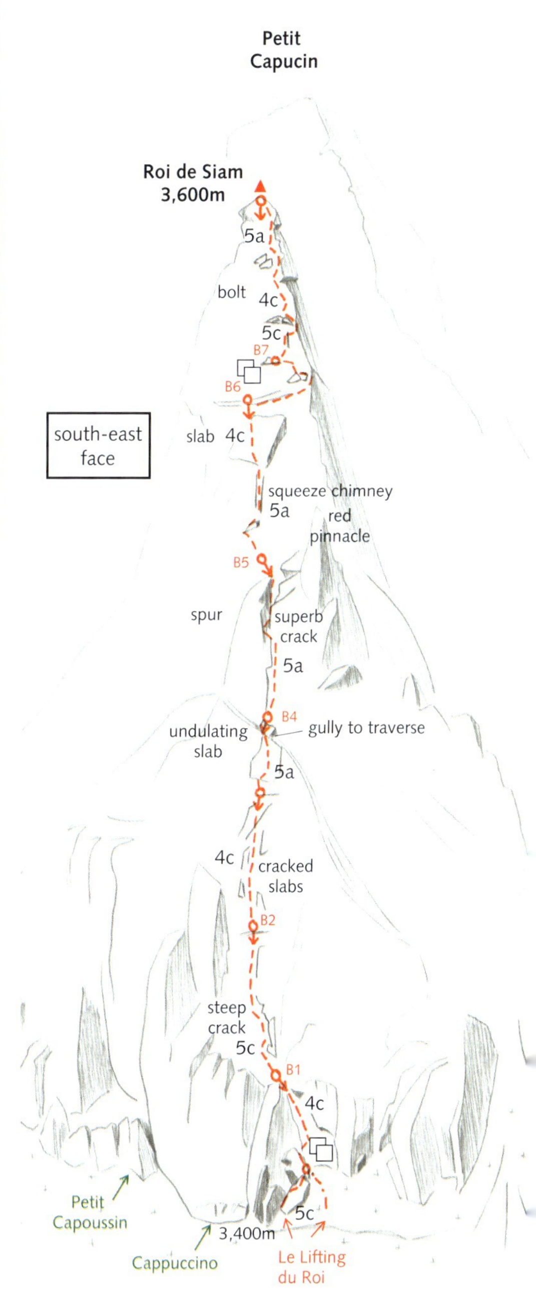

TOUR RONDE (3,792M)

EAST FACE: BERNEZAT SPUR (3,635M)

START POINT: Pointe Helbronner (3,462m) or the Torino Hut (3,371m). Direct cable car access from Italy or reached from France by traversing the Vallée Blanche (2½ hrs or gondola). See pages 94–95.
DIFFICULTY: TD-, 5c oblig. P3 and P4 are sustained. An A0 or 6b+ overhanging crack. Glacier approach and mountain atmosphere. *In situ* protection on the crux, easy to place nuts and cams. Bolt and chain belays.
TIMES: approach 40 mins; route 2–3 hrs; abseils 1¼ hrs; return to Helbronner 50 mins.
VERTICAL HEIGHT: 200m
CONDITIONS: quickly dry at the beginning of the season, but cracks can remain icy after snowfall. Sun until 2.30 p.m. at the end of July.
GEAR: crampons, ice axe, ice screws, nuts, cams 2–4.
FIRST ASCENT: J.-L. Bernezat & C. Collomb, 17 June 1962.

Bathed in early morning sun, the *Bernezat Spur* climbs the east flank of the Tour Ronde, perched on the cusp between the verdant slopes of the Aosta Valley and the icy ocean of the Vallée Blanche. This position has its demands, and solid route-finding skills are needed to find a way through the huge, square-cut blocks at the base of the pillar, linking weaknesses to weave a way to a steep but very climbable wide crack. Thank you, Bernouze, for this beautiful route, climbed before you heeded the siren call of the desert ...

Rather than continuing along the ridge of poor rock to the summit, we would suggest climbing without a rucksack and abseiling down the route – different times, different ethics.

APPROACH

From Pointe Helbronner, go to the Col des Flambeaux, then head westwards down the slope below the Col and the Aiguille de Toule to a plateau at about 3,300m. Head west, then south, to go up the first part of the valley below the Col d'Entrèves. At around 3,400m, head west to the foot of the spur and its bergschrund (approx. 3,430m). 40 mins. Scramble up to B0, where you can leave boots and sacks.

Notes: P1 is an uninviting pile of stacked blocks but it is not as bad as it looks!

Nuts are needed to back up the doubtful *in situ* cams at the start and end of P4.

DESCENT:

Abseil down the route, then retrace your steps back to Helbronner. 50 mins.

The 'Bernouze' on the east flank of the Tour Ronde.

18

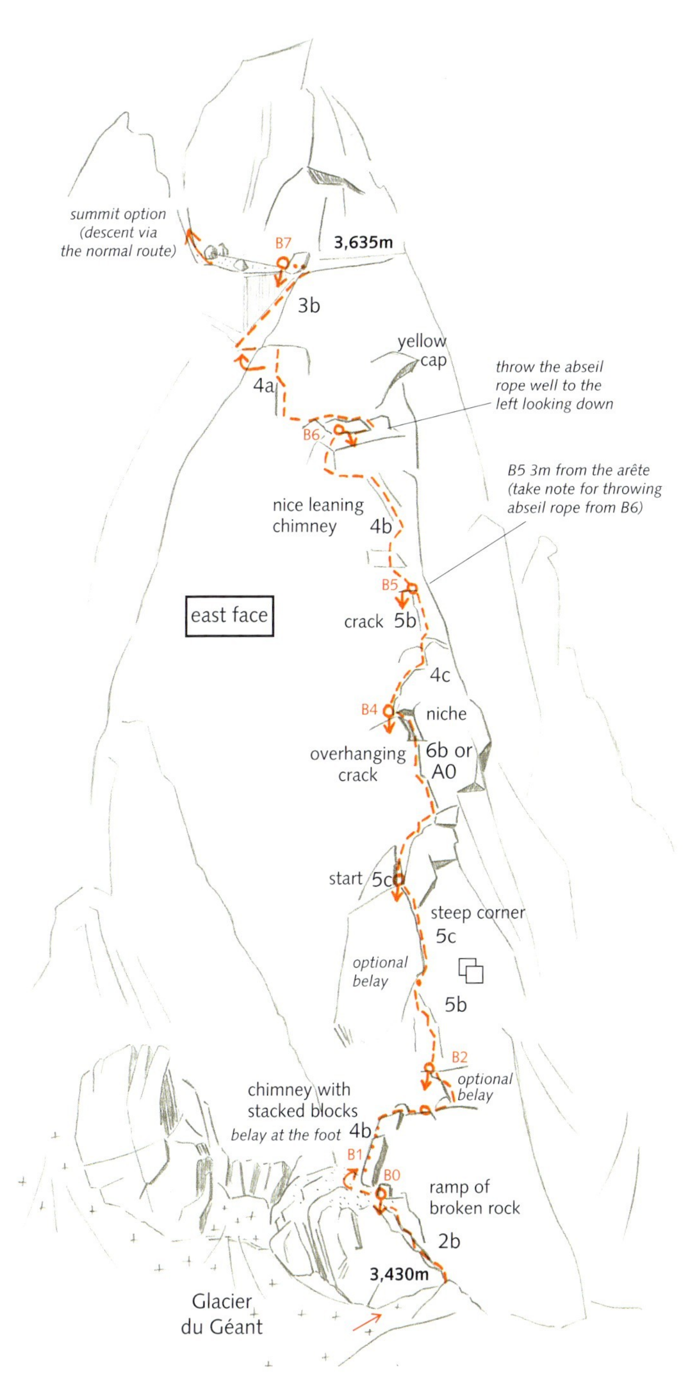
summit option
(descent via
the normal route)
B7
3,635m
3b
yellow
cap
throw the abseil
rope well to the
left looking down
4a
B6
B5 3m from the arête
(take note for throwing
abseil rope from B6)
nice leaning
chimney
4b
B5
east face
crack
5b
4c
B4
niche
overhanging
crack
6b or
A0
start
5c
steep corner
5c
optional
belay
5b
B2
optional
belay
chimney with
stacked blocks
belay at the foot
4b
B1
B0
ramp of
broken rock
2b
3,430m
Glacier
du Géant

AIGUILLE D'ENTRÈVES (3,600M)

TRAVERSE, AND WEST FACE: SALLUARD ROUTE, RÊVES D'ENTRÈVES

START POINT: Pointe Helbronner (3,462m) or the Torino Hut (3,371m). Direct cable car access from Italy or reached from France by traversing the Vallée Blanche (2½ hrs or gondola). See pages 94–95.

The traverse of the Aiguille d'Entrèves is an excellent introduction to Alpine climbing, as it combines a glacier approach with a jagged ridge that calls upon a full range of basic mountaineering techniques.

Seen from afar, the west face doesn't look much, a little stump emerging from the snowy swell, but the closer you get, the steeper it looks and the more tempting it is to climb. So keep going, read the guidebook to decide between the *Salluard* and *Rêves d'Entrèves*, but, above all, be patient and wait for the sun to come round, so you can fully appreciate the superbly coloured rock in its grandiose setting.

SOUTH-WEST–NORTH-EAST TRAVERSE

DIFFICULTY: AD-, 5a, 3c oblig. Exposed. Some mixed ground. Some *in situ* protection and possible to place spike runners (slings). Glacier approach.

TIMES: approach 1 hr; traverse 2–3 hrs; return to Helbronner 45 mins.

VERTICAL HEIGHT: 80m.

CONDITIONS: a little snow can make the route more entertaining.

GEAR: crampons, ice axe, ice screws, nuts, cams.

FIRST ASCENTS: *South-West Ridge*: L. Enzenhofer, L.V. Hibbler & R. Weitzenböck, 22 July 1913. *North-East Ridge*: A. Hess, F. Santi & J. Proment, 31 August 1897.

APPROACH

From Helbronner, go over the Col des Flambeaux and traverse below the north face of the Aiguille de Toule. Turn left (south-west then south) and go up the combe to the Col d'Entrèves.

ASCENT

Start by climbing easy blocks on the left of the ridge. Continue to the summit by following the crest of the ridge, on either its right side or its left side, as the terrain dictates – descend a chimney, climb another chimney (3c), a fin, and a steep wall (5b) just before the summit.

DESCENT

From the summit, go down a short corner on the north side to a peg in a wall on the right. Abseil or climb down for 50m to a notch. Go left round an arête and cross a cracked slab to a rib, which is followed for around 100m. The next crest is climbed on the right for two pitches and then on the left. A short descent on the Italian (east) side leads to a small saddle. Follow the track (north-west) back under the Aiguille d'Entrèves to join the approach route.

WEST FACE ROUTES

DIFFICULTY: D+ to TD-. Some fixed gear. *In situ* abseil stations. Glacier approach.

TIMES: approach 50 mins; routes 2 hrs; abseils 40 mins; return 45 mins.

VERTICAL HEIGHT: 130m.

CONDITIONS: even steep west faces have cracks and ledges that hold the snow. The area around the col can be quite windy. Gets the afternoon sun.

GEAR: crampons, ice axe, ice screws, nuts, cams 1–3, perhaps a few pegs (knife-blades and large corners, hammer), gear for backing up belays and replacing abseil slings.

FIRST ASCENTS: *Salluard*: M.T. & T. Busi, M. & C. Fuselli, F. & Franco Salluard, 17 August 1952. *Rêves d'Entrèves*: N. d'Albrand & O. Ratheaux, 7 August 1991.

APPROACH

As for the traverse but just before the Col d'Entrèves bear left (east) and go up to the bergschrund, directly below the summit. 50 mins.

SALLUARD ROUTE

D+, 5a oblig. Cracks and corners with a spectacular finish on the summit ridge. The rock in the first section requires care. *In situ* belays and some *in situ* protection, nuts and cams required.

DESCENT

Abseil down *Rêves d'Entrèves* or descend the north-east ridge (PD, may need crampons).

RÊVES D'ENTRÈVES

TD-, 6a oblig. Nice, direct line to the summit. Steep climbing on a succession of slabs and clean-cut cracks. Widely spaced *in situ* protection.

Notes: B0 on nuts/cams. P1: no *in situ* gear but easy to protect and with good rests. P2: steep and bold start but can be avoided by moving on to the *Salluard Route*.

DESCENT

Abseil down the route.

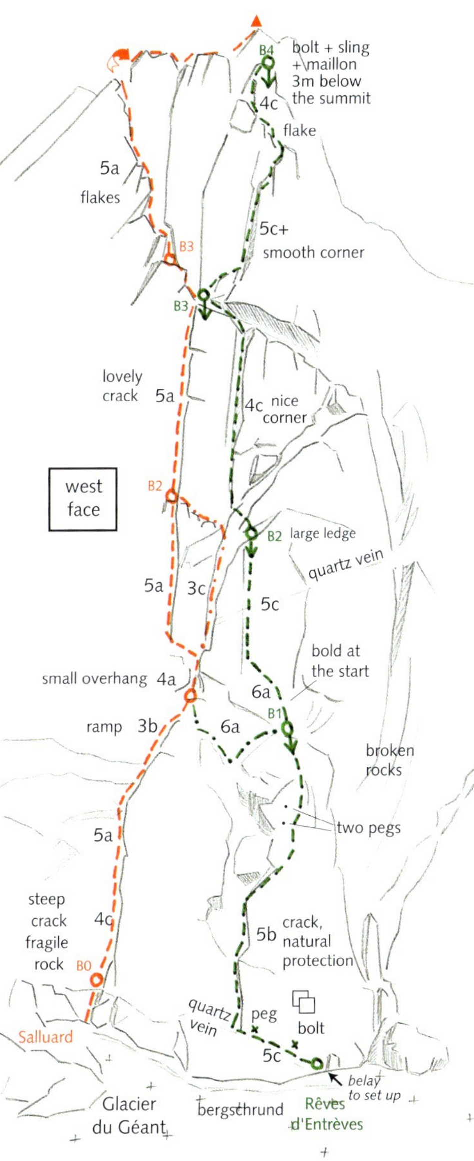

DENT DU GÉANT (4,013M)

WEST FACE: NORMAL ROUTE, GÉANT BRANCHÉ

START POINT: Pointe Helbronner (3,462m) or the Torino Hut (3,371m). Direct cable car access from Italy or reached from France by traversing the Vallée Blanche (2½ hrs or gondola). See pages 94–95.
TIMES: approach 2 hrs; climbs 2 hrs; abseils 30 mins; + 1½ hrs back to Helbronner.
VERTICAL HEIGHT: 620m including 150m of rock climbing.
CONDITIONS: as soon as the snow has melted, generally in summer because of the altitude. Wait for the sun to come round before starting climbing. Dangerous in stormy weather.
GEAR: crampons, ice axe, ice screws, long slings, nuts, cams 2–3, warm clothing.
FIRST ASCENTS: *Normal Route*: J.-J., B. & D. Maquignaz, 28 July 1882. *Géant Branché*: C. Bodin & O. Ratheaux, 4 August 1990.

Climbing the Dent du Géant is always hugely satisfying if you are well prepared. That means being fit and acclimatised, and being able to climb grade 5, if you intend to do the *Normal Route*.

Géant Branché avoids the traffic jams on the *Normal Route* and includes one of the best corner pitches in the massif, but the climbing is much more difficult. In addition, it requires placing natural protection and backing up the belays, because the fixed gear is no longer reliable.

After a surreal moment on the summit aerie, at the feet of the Virgin Mary with her lightning-pierced forehead, a rapid descent via the abseil line on the south face lands you almost at the foot of the route.

APPROACH

From Helbronner, traverse north-east until just to the north of the Col du Géant. Go past the foot of the Aiguilles Marbrées and continue up the Glacier du Géant to the foot of a gully on the left that goes up through the lower buttresses directly below the Dent (1 hr). Cross the bergschrund and climb the gully (or the rock on its right bank).

Exit on to a shoulder, then bear right across broken rocks, often mixed with snow. Head north-east alongside the rocky ridge to the yellow pinnacles, which are turned easily on their right (slight descent on the south face before going back up) to get to the Salle à Manger (1 hr). Traverse left across the snowfield to gain the south-west corner of the Dent (platform on which to gear up and leave sacks).

E pericoloso sporgersi!

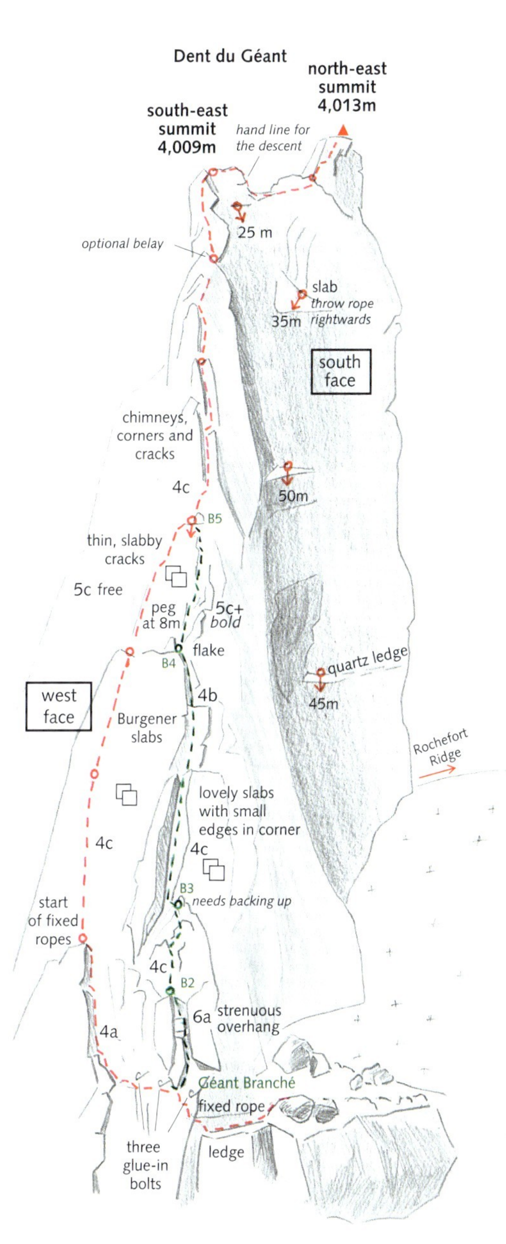

DENT DU GÉANT
WEST FACE: NORMAL ROUTE, GÉANT BRANCHÉ

DESCENT
Three or four abseils down the south face to get back to the platform. The belays on the *Normal Route* are also equipped for abseiling. Follow the approach route back to Helbronner (1½ hrs).

The Burgener slabs, 4c max ...

NORMAL ROUTE
AD+, 4c oblig. 5c if you don't use the fixed ropes. Exposed climbing at altitude. It is less tiring to climb the rock than to pull on the ropes.

GÉANT BRANCHÉ
TD, 6a oblig. if you do the original start and the bold finish (both can be avoided). Effects of altitude. Widely spaced and ageing *in situ* gear.

Notes: Set up B1 at the glue-in bolt (the *Normal Route* heads left, whereas *Géant Branché* goes up right above the first bolt). The overhang on P2 can feel difficult before you are warmed up. Apart from the bold start to P5, the rest is more classic. P4 is 52m long. Take a very long sling for the flake at B4. P5 is quite bold before the first runner, a peg. A bolt would make this section safer and make the route more balanced; in the meantime, it can be avoided by climbing the *Normal Route*, just to the left.

The magnificent corner (4c).

20

PARETE DEI TITANI (2,131M) MONTS ROUGES DE TRIOLET (2,800M)

PARETE DEI TITANI: GÉNÉPI ROUTES

START POINT: Arnouva car park (1,769m) in the Italian Val Ferret, 30km from Chamonix.
DIFFICULTY: D, 6a, 5c oblig. Well-protected slab climbing. *In situ* abseil stations.
TIMES: approach 45 mins; routes 2 hrs; abseils 45 mins.
VERTICAL HEIGHT: 250m
CONDITIONS: dries quickly thanks to its moderate altitude and sunny aspect.

The Paroi des Titans is next to the path to the Dalmazzi Hut. It has three nice routes: *Vénus* is 6b, *Génépi 1* and *2* are easier, involving pleasant grade-5 climbing. The granite is superb and is well worth the trip through the Mont Blanc Tunnel. What's more, being on the south side of the massif, it is often dry when it is raining in Chamonix.

APPROACH

45 mins, following the path to the Dalmazzi Hut. See page 94.

MONTS ROUGES DE TRIOLET, POINTE 2,800M: CRIS-TAL AND EL CATALAN

START POINT: Dalmazzi (or Triolet) Hut (2,590m), 2½ hrs from the Italian Val Ferret. See page 94.
DIFFICULTY: AD, 5c oblig. Slabs. Very well bolted. Rock is lichenous in places. *El Catalan* is a three-pitch variation start, 5c+.
TIMES: approach 2 mins; route 2 hrs; abseils 45 mins.
VERTICAL HEIGHT: 230m
CONDITIONS: the routes dry quickly and get the sun at around 9 a.m. in summer.
FIRST ASCENTS: *Cris-Tal*: M. Bernini, D. Gonella & S. Latino, September 2007; *El Catalan*: M. Bernini & M. Bianchi, 23 July 2008.

The Parete dei Titani at the foot of the Monts Rouges. The *Génépi* routes are shown in red.

Inset: The Dalmazzi Hut.

DALMAZZI

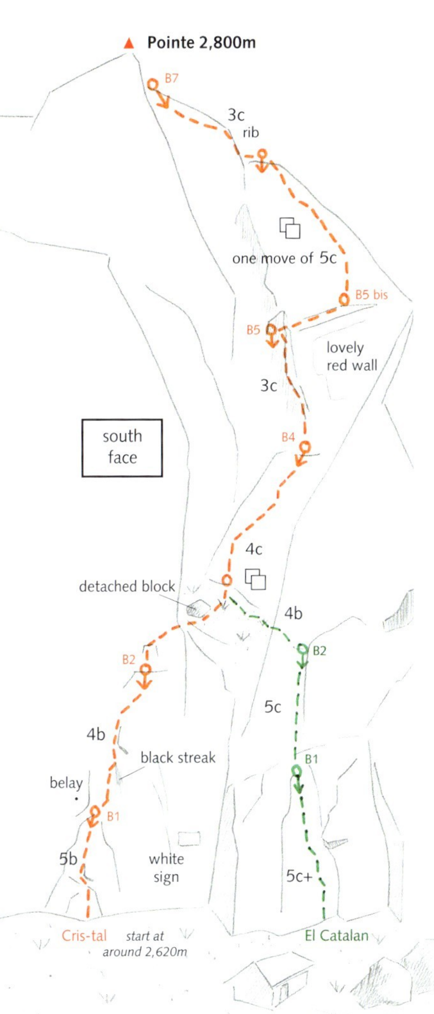

P4 of *Génépi* (5c).

Just a stone's throw from the hut, *Cris-tal* is an excellent introduction to the area. It is also a good way of saving a day of uncertain weather, as the slabby climbing is very enjoyable and it is possible to abseil off at any point. For beginners, the rock provides plenty of opportunities for learning to place natural protection while climbing safely, thanks to the bolts and bombproof belays. And it all faces due south ...

APPROACH:

Two minutes, just behind the hut's toilets!

DESCENT

Abseil down the route.

MONTS ROUGES DE TRIOLET – CENTRAL SUMMIT (3,327M)

SOUTH-WEST FACE: LA BÉRÉSINA

START POINT: Dalmazzi (or Triolet) Hut (2,590m), 2½ hrs from the Italian Val Ferret. See page 94.
DIFFICULTY: D+, 5c oblig. Big wall feel. Remote. Good route-finding skills needed on some of the pitches. Bolts widely spaced but easy to place nuts and cams. *In situ* belays (abseils). Steep snowfield. Bergschrund sometimes difficult to cross.
TIMES: approach 1½ hrs; route 3 hrs; descent 2 hrs to the foot of the route.
VERTICAL HEIGHT: 300m.
CONDITIONS: this west-facing wall tends to get the brunt of any storms, which arrive quickly and fiercely. Precipitation often falls as hail due to the altitude. Gets the sun around 10 a.m. in summer.
GEAR: crampons and ice axe (left at the foot of the route), nuts, cams 1–3.
FIRST ASCENT: E. Lanza, M. Motto & M. Piola, 3 September 1995.

You hear the name more and more, but where is it? People say 'Dalmazzi' with such a knowing air ... It's very simple. Go through the Mont Blanc Tunnel to Val Ferret, and the Dalmazzi Hut is up there, in the Triolet basin.

The *Bérésina* wall, hidden at the end of the moraine, is quite a slog to get to. A route like this could not have been found by just anyone ... Manlio Motto loves beautiful lines where you have to seek out the holds and read the rock, not just scrabble to the next bolt come what may. As a result, the spacing between the bolts can be a little intimidating. The abseils are not easy, either, and tend to try and keep you on the face, even though your mind is already enjoying the hospitality back at the hut.

Abseiling down the hanging corner.

DALMAZZI

APPROACH

From the hut, follow the path north-west to the left-bank moraine of the Glacier de Triolet. Go up the moraine to around 2,870m. The route, on the south-west pillar of the central summit, opposite the icefall, comes into view just before you enter the upper cirque.

Two rock islands emerge from the snowfield to the north-east. Go past the foot of the first island and up the steep slope.

START

Approx. 15m right of the big corner with a tongue of snow at the bottom (pink-ish rock). The slings at B0 can be seen above the snowfield (height will depend on the snow cover). It is often easier to start on the left. An intermediate belay can be taken on a short sling at the bergschrund. From here, traverse right easily (3b, nut protection) for 20m to a belay on a platform, where you can leave all the heavy glacier gear.

DESCENT

Climb back down the summit pitch, then abseil down the route. Take care during the first three abseils as ropes tend to jam.

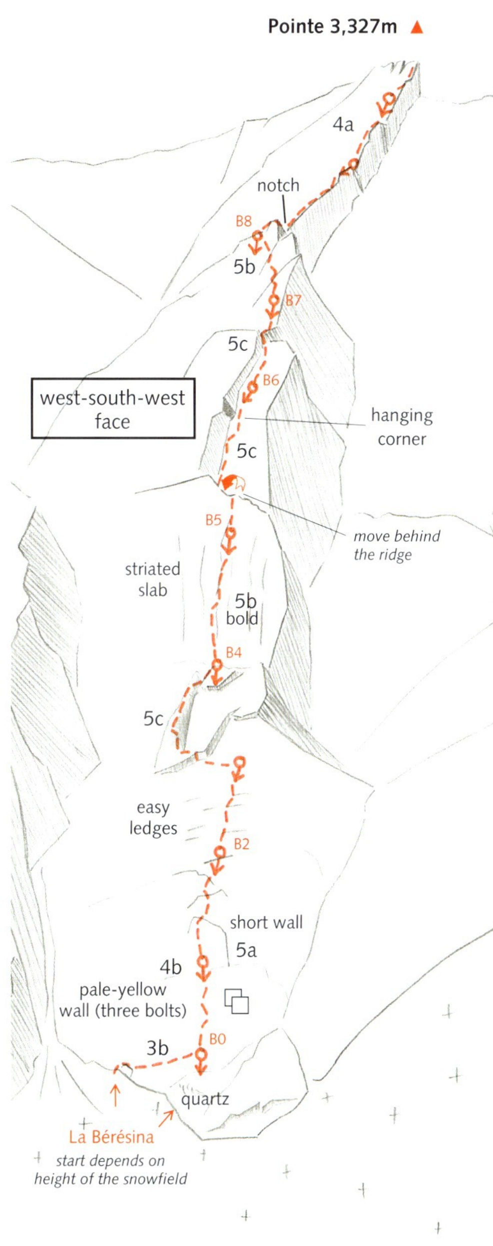

MONTS ROUGES DE TRIOLET – SECOND CENTRAL SUMMIT (3,289M)

SOUTH-WEST PILLAR: PROFUMO PROIBITO

START POINT: Dalmazzi (or Triolet) Hut (2,590m), 2½ hrs from the Italian Val Ferret. See page 94.
DIFFICULTY: TD-, 6a oblig. for the slab, the rest is 5/5c cracks. Quite well bolted (including belays/abseils) except for B0, where there is no fixed gear. Unusually steep for granite.
TIMES: approach 1½ hrs; route 3 hrs; descent 1 hr back to the foot of the route.
VERTICAL HEIGHT: 200m.
CONDITIONS: the steep and exposed pillar dries quickly after rain. Gets the sun around 10 a.m. in summer.
GEAR: crampons and ice axe may be needed early in the season. A few nuts and cams.
FIRST ASCENT: Gisa & Manlio Motto, 28 August 1994.

Profumo Proibito is the area's great classic at the grade. Climbing the left edge of the imposing Red Tower, which soars like a rocket into the sky, it follows a steep, obvious and beautiful line. However, it is a route that is quickly tamed if you are on form, as the rock is exceptional and the bolts alternate well with nuts and cams. It is the approach that requires care, as the morning mist has caused more than one rock athlete to go astray in the search for the grail.

APPROACH

Follow the path north-west from the hut. At a fork in the path at 2,600m, just after a streambed (5 mins from the hut), take the right-hand (uphill) branch. Two minutes later (2,610m, cairn), turn right (north-east) on to a steep path that meanders up the grass. This allows you to go very high above the cliffs in order to traverse north when the grass runs out (scree and cairns). Just before the ridge that comes down from the second central summit (where the route *Kermesse Folk* starts, bolt with a sling 5m from the ground), bear right through the blocks to the foot of a ramp that leads to the approach to *Profumo* (large cairn, approx. 2,740m, 30 mins). Climb this easy ramp for 25m (belay on the left), then follow a reasonably well-marked path with cairns that inscribes a gigantic inverted Z (right-left-right) for about 250m. At the entrance to a small cirque, zigzag upwards and leftwards to get to a large ledge at the foot of *Profumo* (approx. 3,000m) by traversing above the precipice (40 mins from the cairn at 2,740m). Beware of rock-fall.

The lovely crack of pitch 4 (5c).

Notes: Do not belay at the foot of the pillar. Climb up to the first bolt, which can be used as a belay, backed up by a nut down and to the left.

DESCENT

Abseil down the route, then go back down the Z.

The pillar of *Profumo*, as seen from the approach.

DALMAZZI

23

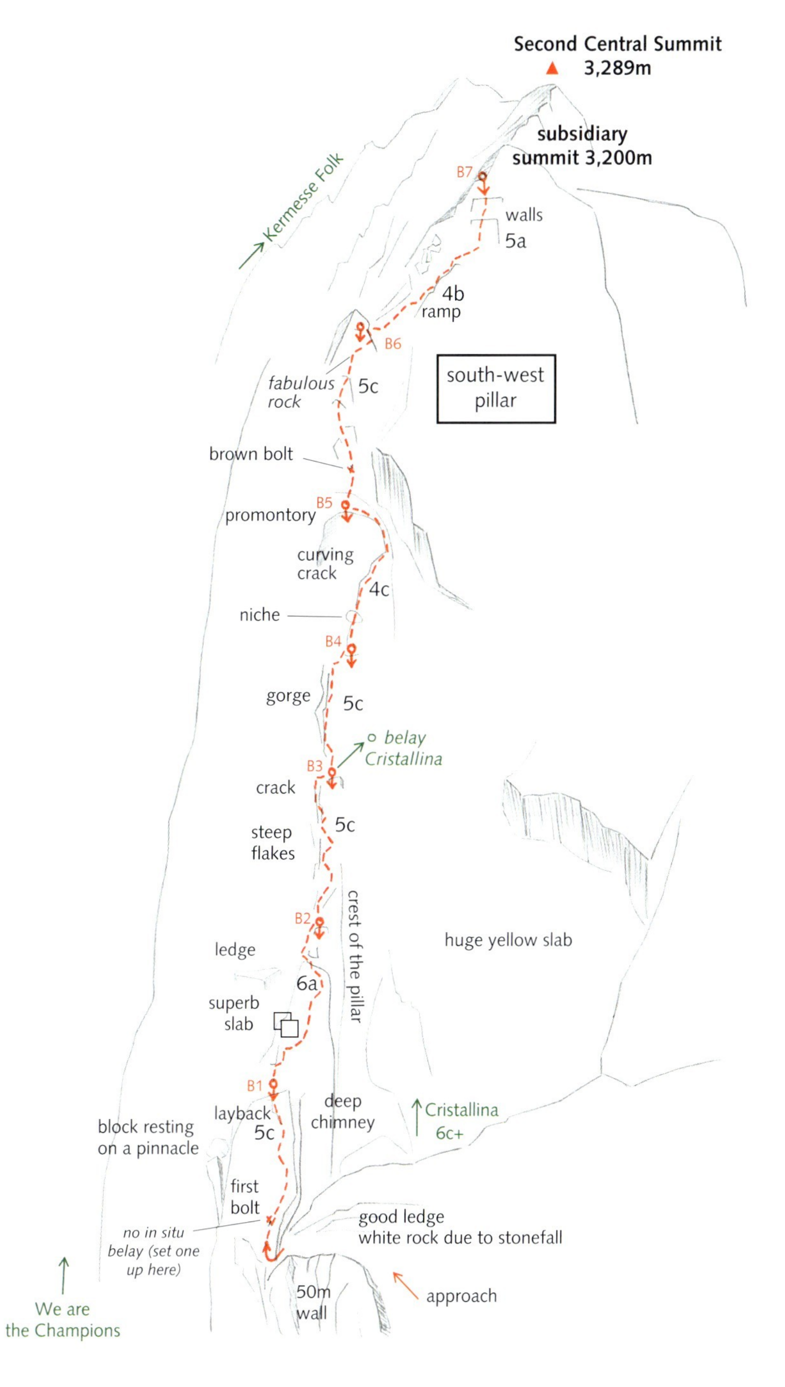
Second Central Summit
3,289m
subsidiary
summit 3,200m
Kermesse Folk
B7
walls
5a
4b
ramp
B6
fabulous
rock
5c
south-west
pillar
brown bolt
B5
promontory
curving
crack
4c
niche
B4
gorge
5c
belay
Cristallina
B3
crack
steep
flakes
5c
crest of the pillar
B2
ledge
huge yellow slab
6a
superb
slab
B1
layback
5c
deep
chimney
Cristallina
6c+
block resting
on a pinnacle
first
bolt
good ledge
white rock due to stonefall
no in situ
belay (set one
up here)
50m
wall
approach
We are
the Champions

THE BRÉVENT (2,525M)

SOUTH FACE: POÈME A LOU. SOUTH-EAST FACE: FRISON-ROCHE ROUTE

START POINT: top station of the Brévent cable car (2,500m). See page 95.

Although the Brévent is best known as a tourist viewpoint, it shouldn't be forgotten that there is a wonderful crag below the cable car. *Poème à Lou* involves intricate climbing on a rare slab of steep and compact gneiss. It is simply superb. The *Frison-Roche* was named in honour of the author of *Premier de Cordée*. Slab climbing on microscopic holds, an archetypal wide crack, and a fabulous corner on the final pitch combine to create the area's great classic.

POÈME A LOU

DIFFICULTY: TD+, 6a+ oblig. Sustained and strenuous with a very fingery overhanging wall. Technical climbing on rock that is difficult to read.
TIMES: approach 25 mins; route 3 hrs.
VERTICAL HEIGHT: 230m
CONDITIONS: snow melts off the south face very quickly, but there is steep snow in the Belin Couloir until late in the season.
GEAR: 14 quickdraws.
FIRST ASCENT: Karen & François Pallandre, 20 June 2003.

APPROACH

From the Brévent, go down to the start of the *Frison-Roche*. Continue down the Belin couloir for about 150m, then bear right to the fixed rope used to swing round on to the south face. Go up slightly to the start of the route, in the middle of the face. 25 mins.

RETURN

Head left up to the Brévent. 5 mins.

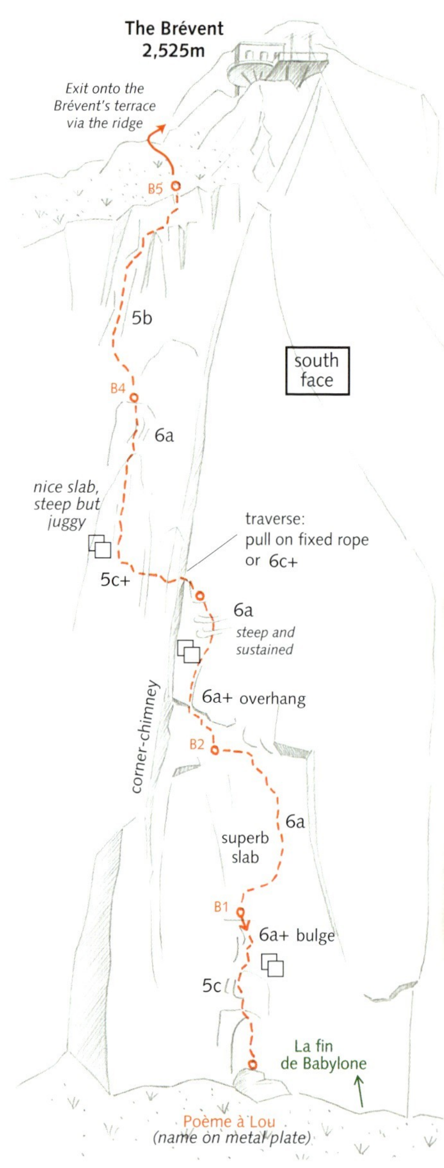

The huge face of the Brévent, high above Chamonix.
Yellow line = *Poème à Lou*, red line = *Frison-Roche*.

The 6a slab on P1.

FRISON-ROCHE ROUTE

DIFFICULTY: TD-, 6a, 5c oblig. Short but technical and quite strenuous.

TIMES: approach 15 mins; climb 2 hrs; return 5 mins.

VERTICAL HEIGHT: 200m.

GEAR: nuts, cams 2–3.

FIRST ASCENT: M. Arizzi, Y. Ancrenaz, A. & G. Payot, & D. Chenevoy, August 2000.

APPROACH

From the Brévent, head north down the track. Go past the single-pitch climbs (south). Continue along the track on the Chamonix side, turning right just after the first bend (large boulders, cairn, 2,380m). A steep path in the upper part of the Belin couloir leads to the ledge at the foot of the route. 15 mins.

Return: go up the ridge to the cable car and summit viewpoint.

LOWER BUTTRESSES OF THE BRÉVENT

SOUTH-WEST FACE: LA SOMONE, CRAKOUKASS

START POINT: top of the Brévent cable car (2,500m). See page 95.
CONDITIONS: quickly snow-free in spring.

The recent new-routing explosion has resulted in the development of many secondary lines on discontinuous buttresses that nevertheless produce coherent 'off-the-peg' climbs. *La Somone* and *Crakoukass* are perfect examples of this. *La Somone* provides a relaxing ramble on perfect gneiss at a reasonable grade; *Crakoukass* is much steeper and includes a strenuous layback that will get the heart going, although it can be aided.

With a downhill approach, numerous bailout options and a short stroll back to the cable car, these routes have everything a crag rat could want.

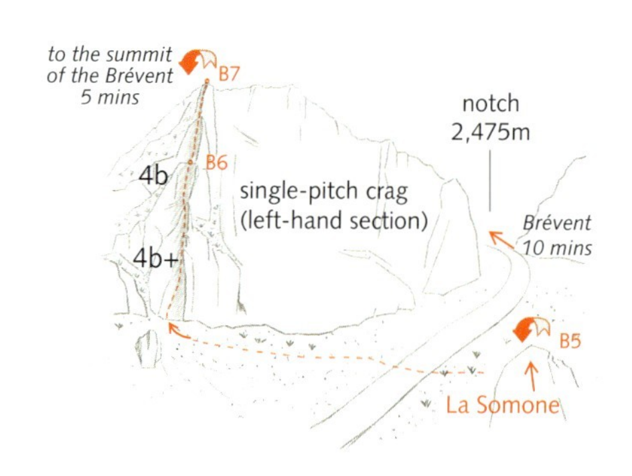

LA SOMONE

DIFFICULTY: D, 5b, 4c oblig. Slabs, corners and cracks. Well bolted.
TIMES: approach 15 mins; route 2½ hrs; return to the cable car 5 mins.
VERTICAL HEIGHT: 200m.
GEAR: rope for a 20m abseil, nuts.
FIRST ASCENT: M. Méot & M. & J. Franc, 13 and 14 August 2001.

APPROACH

Head north down the track from the Brévent. Go past the notch at 2,457m and continue along the track on the south face. After the second hairpin, traverse left across scree slopes to the start of the route (sling on a thread).

Crakoukass, including the upper buttresses.

Notes: The final wall is quite a distance from the rest of the route, on the west pillar of the left-hand section of the Brévent's single-pitch crag.

Return to the Brévent cable car via the north ridge of this summit.

CRAKOUKASS

DIFFICULTY: D+, 6b, 5c oblig. Balanced series of pitches apart from a 6b crack (A0 or escape off the route). Well bolted except for B3 (poor bolts, take a sling to put round the pillar).
TIMES: approach 20 mins; route 3 hrs; return to the Brévent 10 mins.
VERTICAL HEIGHT: 250m.
GEAR: long slings, a few nuts.
FIRST ASCENT: M. Méot, P. Manrard & J. Balmat, July 2000.

APPROACH

Follow the track past the start of *La Somone*. When the path turns north-east (towards Planpraz), the foot of the route can be seen a few metres above on the left.

Notes: Instead of going back up the track after the final gendarme, it is possible to climb the last section of *La Somone*.

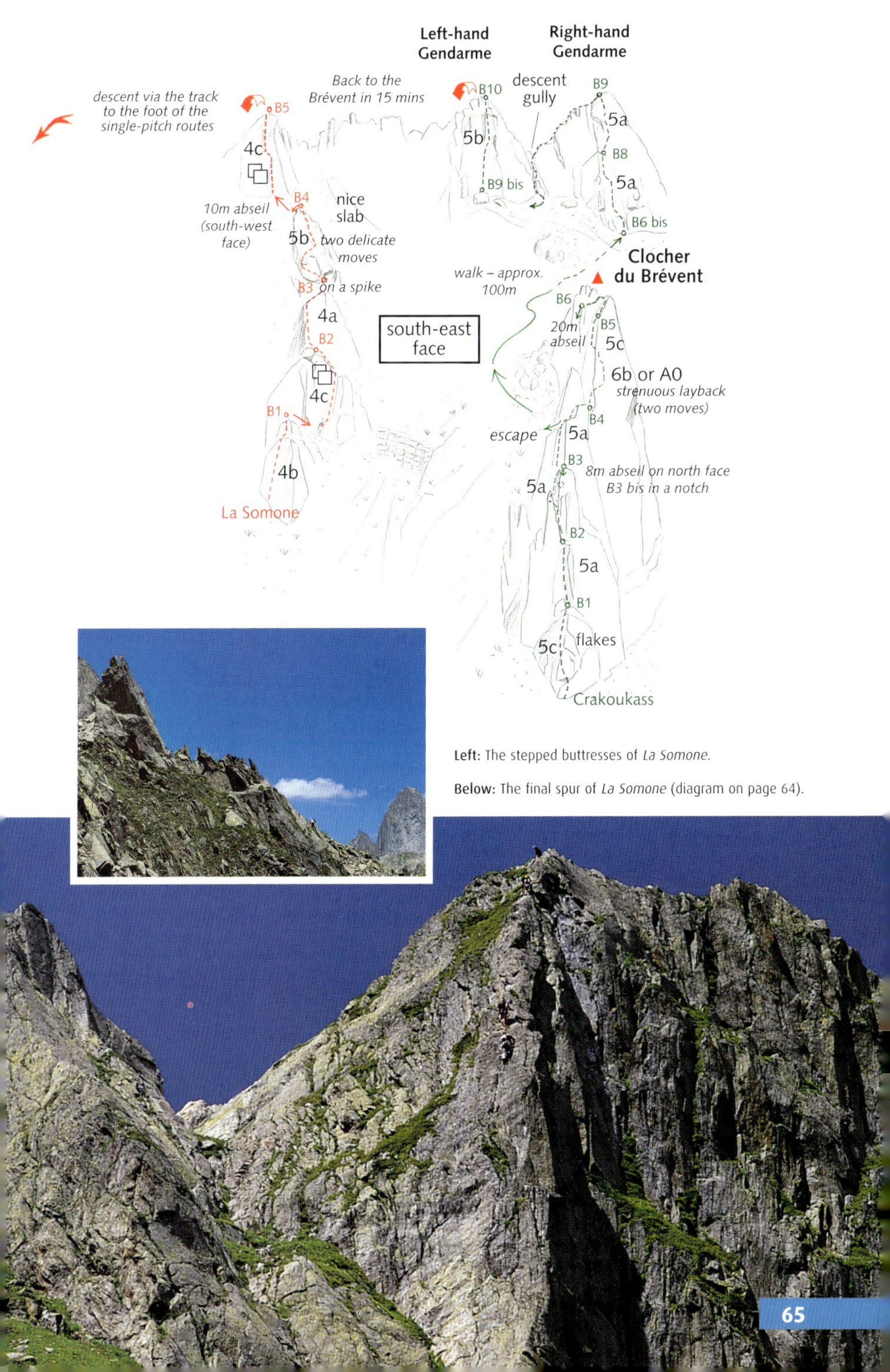

Left: The stepped buttresses of *La Somone*.

Below: The final spur of *La Somone* (diagram on page 64).

CLOCHER DE PLANPRAZ (2,412M)

SOUTH FACE: COCHER-COCHON

START POINT: Planpraz (1,999m), midway station of the Brévent cable car. See page 95.

DIFFICULTY: D+, 6a, 5c oblig. Varied climbing. Last two pitches are sustained and exposed.

TIMES: approach 35 mins; route 3 hrs; descent 30 mins.

VERTICAL HEIGHT: 270m.

CONDITIONS: the snowfields melt quickly, including those in the approach cirque. Lichen on the lower part of the route takes time to dry after rain.

GEAR: rope for a 35m abseil.

FIRST ASCENT: M. Méot & C. Mussat, with J. & M. Franc, 19 August 2000.

Describing a new climb is a creative act in which the name is all-important. Manu Méot gets as much pleasure from devising playful paronyms as he does from doing new routes. In this case, he imagines a crude coachman (cocher-cochon) cavorting from campanile (clocher) to pinnacle. Honni soit qui mal y pense!

The south face of the Clocher hides many surprises. Although the lower sections are a little vegetated, the rock on the spurs is clean and the climbing improves as you gain height. On the final pitch, a cool head and a determined approach are needed to cope with the exposure and win the day.

APPROACH

From the cable car station at Planpraz, head north-west then north to the junction with the path to Lac Cornu. Follow this path for about 20 mins, then head north-west up the steep cirque below the Clocher de Planpraz (faint path and cairns) to the start of the route, on the right-hand side of the wall. 35 mins.

DESCENT

A 35m abseil down the west side of the summit leads to the Col du Clocher. Follow the obvious path (cairns) south back to Planpraz. 30 mins.

At the foot of the final buttress.

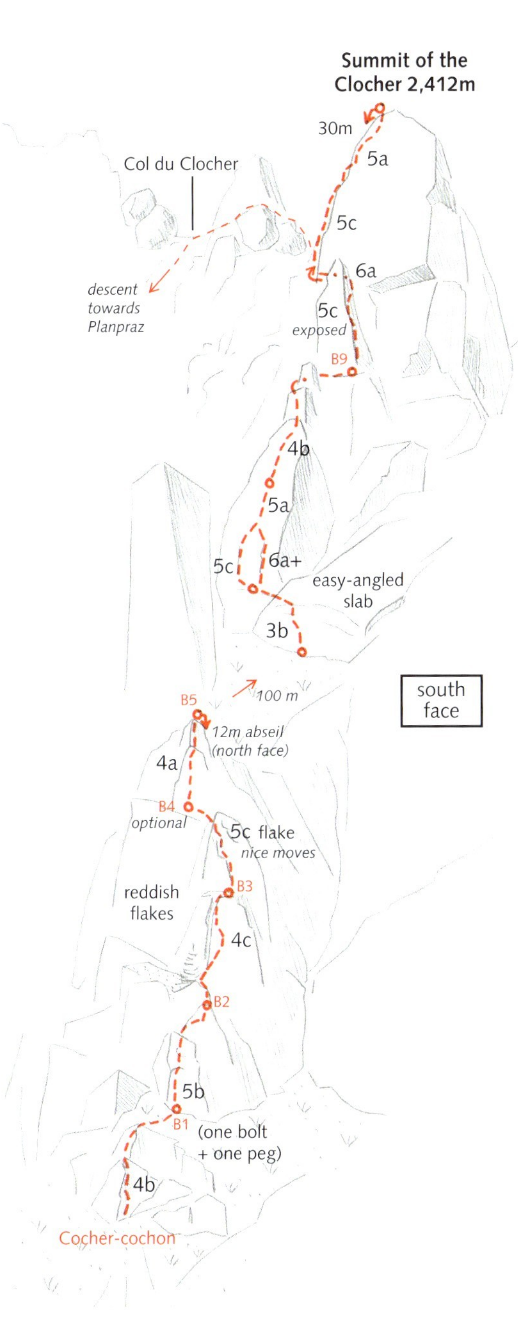

A complex face but with excellent climbing.

AIGUILLE DE L'INDEX (2,595M)

SOUTH-WEST FACE: L'AN D'ÉMILE. EAST FACE: SOUTH-EAST RIDGE, PERROUX ROUTE. LOWER BUTTRESS OF THE GLIÈRE: MANI PULITI & NEZ ROUGE

START POINT: the Index (2,396m), top of the chairlift reached from La Flégère. See page 95.

Three routes, three grades, three characters, all on the most popular peak in the Aiguilles Rouges.

The *South-East Ridge* of this archetypal needle is ideal terrain for novice climbers to put into practice techniques learnt on smaller crags, although it can sometimes feel very exposed, especially the abseil from the summit.

The *Perroux Route*, named after one of ice climbing's great pioneers, climbs the middle of the east face. Here, a steady approach is required in order to savour the technical moves on unusual rock.

Partially hidden and often overlooked, the south-west face can appear very intimidating, especially early in the day, before the sun has come round to temper the ambience. On *L'An d'Émile*, the rock is steep and the climbing is intricate but never excessively difficult.

SOUTH-WEST FACE: L'AN D'ÉMILE

DIFFICULTY: TD, 6a, 5c oblig. Steep and sustained. P3, P4 and P7 are hard to read. Few cracks for nuts and cams but well bolted except for the upper section of P7.
TIMES: approach 30 mins; route 2 hrs; descent 30 mins.
VERTICAL HEIGHT: 250m
CONDITIONS: gets the sun at around 10.30 a.m. in summer.
GEAR: nuts.
FIRST ASCENT: K. & F. Pallandre, 12 July 2001.

APPROACH

Head south from the Index chairlift to pass below the east face of the Index. Go down the top part of the Combe Lachenal, then turn south-west on to the path to the Col de la Glière. After a short distance, turn off the path and go up the gully on the south-west edge of the Index for about 200m. Move right on to a ledge at the foot of a reddish slab at the start of the route (bolts visible). 30 mins.

DESCENT

See *South-East Ridge*.

SOUTH-EAST RIDGE

DIFFICULTY: AD-, 5a, 4b oblig. Exposed with a lot of traverses. *In situ* belays. Some *in situ* protection but requires nuts and cams. Slightly technical and airy abseil. Descent gully sometimes full of snow.
TIMES: approach 20 mins; route 1 hr; descent 30 mins.
VERTICAL HEIGHT: 150m.
CONDITIONS: May to October, as soon as the snow has melted.
GEAR: crampons/ice axe sometimes needed early in the season (descent), rope for 40m abseil, nuts, cams 0.5–3.
FIRST ASCENT: A. Agussol, H. Bonin, M. Damesme & J. & T. de Lépiney, 16 August 1913.

APPROACH

From the top of the chairlift, head west to the scree slope below the Col de l'Index. Go up the scree to the ledge on the left that divides the face in two. The starting flake is at the end of the ledge. 20 mins.

DESCENT

Do a 40m abseil from just below the north-west side of the summit to a few metres above the Col de l'Index. Go down the gully and the scree slope below the Col to get back to the chairlift. 30 mins.

EAST FACE: PERROUX ROUTE

DIFFICULTY: D, 5a oblig. The original finish (6a+) can be avoided. Mostly slabs and walls with flat holds. Polished rock in places. *In situ* protection of variable quality. All belays *in situ*.
TIMES: approach 10 mins; route 2½ hrs; descent 30 mins.
VERTICAL HEIGHT: 250m.
CONDITIONS: gets the early morning sun.
FIRST ASCENT: J.-C. Brunat & G. Perroux, 1985.

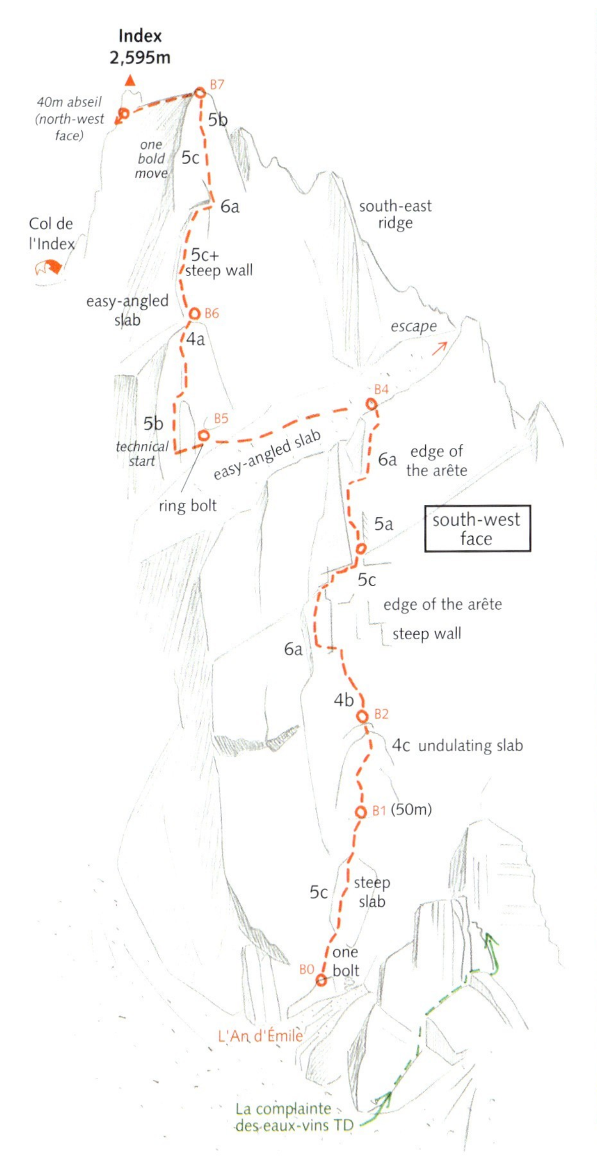

The hidden west face.

L'An d'Émile, the superb wall on P7 (5c+).

APPROACH

Head south to the top of Combe Lachenal, then go north-west up a small scree slope towards the middle of the lower buttress of the face, directly below a small triangular roof, 10m up the wall. The first bolt is on a green slab. 10 mins.

DESCENT

See *South-East Ridge*.

Continued ...

AIGUILLE DE L'INDEX
LOWER BUTTRESS OF THE GLIÈRE

MANI PULITI & NEZ ROUGE

The lower buttress of the Glière, next to the Index, houses two lovely routes, *Mani Puliti* and *Nez Rouge* – six pitches of well-bolted slab climbing, never harder than 5b, on good rock and with spacious belays. What is more, they finish on a beautiful summit, guarded by ibex, opposite Mont Blanc.

APPROACH

For *Mani Puliti,* head west from the chairlift along a ridge of boulders that leads to the foot of the spur (sometimes snow), red dot. 15 mins.

Nez Rouge starts at a light-coloured slab on the right-hand side of the buttress. Bolts clearly visible.

DESCENT

Go down grassy slopes, then follow the path back leftwards to the foot of the buttress.

First ascents: *Mani Puliti*: M. Piola, 23 August 1999; *Nez Rouge*: M. Méot & J. Cellier, 1 September 1998.

Nez Rouge, P1 (5b).

Mani Puliti and *Nez Rouge*, in front of the Index and Mont Blanc.

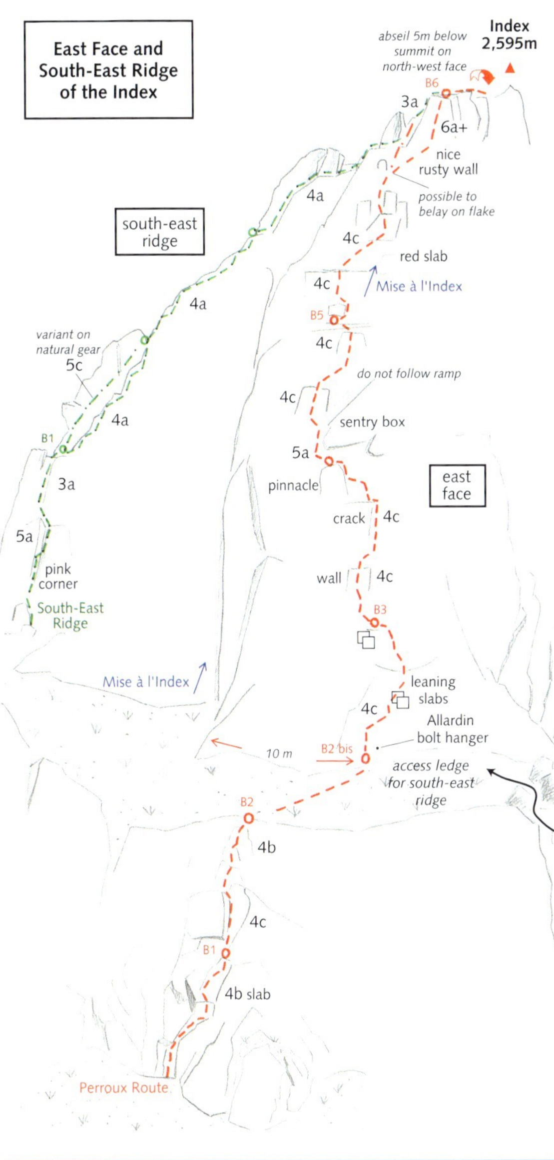

The last pitch of the *Perroux Route* (6a+).

Approaching the top of the *South-East Ridge*.

AIGUILLE DU POUCE (2,874M)

SOUTH FACE: VOIE DES DALLES

START POINT: top of the Index chairlift (2,396m), reached from La Flégère. See page 95.
DIFFICULTY: TD-, 5c oblig. Long route. Mostly cracks. Sustained lower section. Retreat difficult after B7. *In situ* gear in poor condition. Nuts and cams required. Snow on the approach and descent.
TIMES: approach 1½ hrs; route 4 to 5 hrs; descent 1½ hrs.
VERTICAL HEIGHT: 400m.
CONDITIONS: sunny aspect so rapidly snow free, but often snow on the approach and descent. Not recommended after rain or in uncertain weather.
GEAR: crampons/ice axe early in the season, long slings, nuts (including several small nuts), cams 0.5–3.
FIRST ASCENT: B. Kintzele, R. Mallon & J. Marutzi, 2 September 1967.

The *Voie des Dalles* is an established classic, a great adventure and an excellent introduction to big Alpine faces. A lower section on excellent rough gneiss is followed by more adventurous terrain where intuition and a little mountain sense are needed to stay on the right line. In addition, the long descent means this is not a route to underestimate.

APPROACH

Looking west-north-west from the Index, a large rock spire (the 'Wehrlin Gendarme') can be seen in the gully of the Glière normal route. Go up snowfields or the rightwards-trending moraine to the foot of this spire, then traverse left (ramp) to the snowfield below the Doigt de la Glière. Go up this snowfield to a saddle to the right of the Doigt (1 hr, view of the Pouce).

It is possible to go straight down from this saddle into the Combe de la Floria, but this is inadvisable, as the slope is often bare ice and subject to stone-fall. It is better to follow the longer but safer route down the west ridge below the shoulder between the Glière and the Doigt (crampons and ice axe depending on snow cover). This also allows you to inspect the face. From the saddle, head left (south) to the rounded crest of the ridge, then go down the large, west-facing valley to the north of the Lacs Noirs (short, easy chimneys at first). Once level with the Pouce (visible on the right), descend northwards, then north-east along a shoulder dotted with small cliffs to get to the Combe de la Floria. Cross the stream at about 2,400m and go up northwards (scree and boulderfield) to the foot of the face (30 mins).

DESCENT

Follow the east ridge, at first on the wide crest, then going to the north of two large gendarmes, well below the crest (climbs and descents). Go past several gendarmes, at first turning them on the left, and then mostly on the right, then traverse across the right flank of a dome of loose rock. A short descent (south) leads to the saddle below the Doigt de la Glière and the approach route. 1½ hrs.

Notes: The 'Guides' Start' (5b), on the right-hand side of the wall, is a more interesting way of starting the route. The left-hand crack on P2 (4a) can be protected with small nuts.

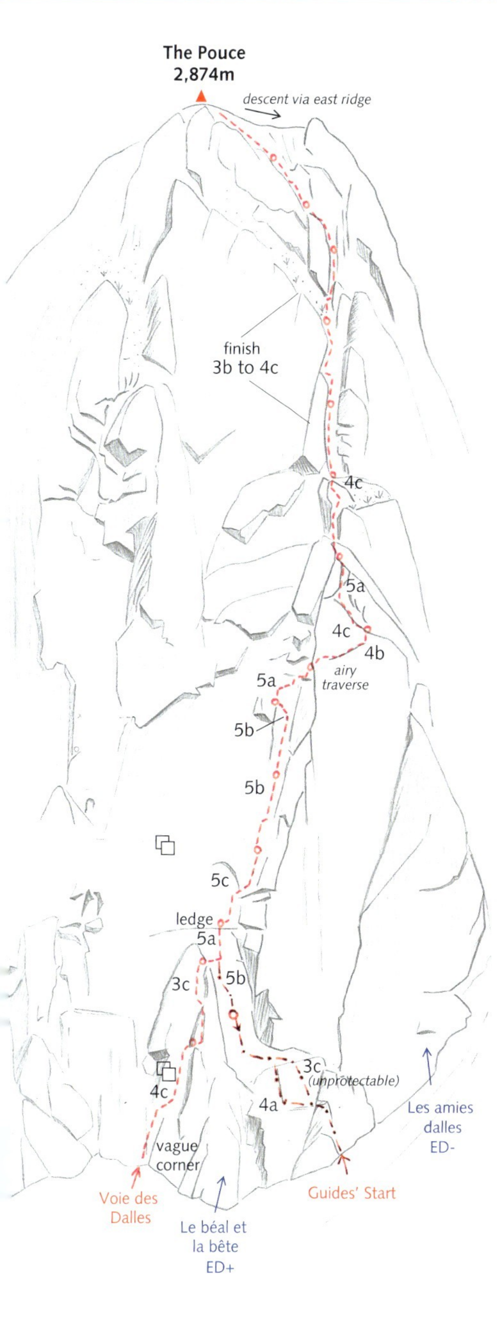

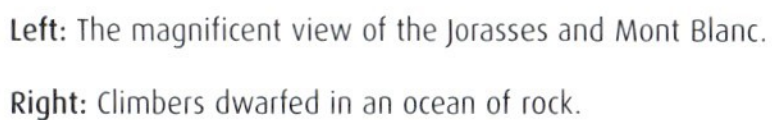

Left: The magnificent view of the Jorasses and Mont Blanc.

Right: Climbers dwarfed in an ocean of rock.

PETITE FLORIA (2,826M)

SOUTH FACE: (MANHATTAN) KABOUL

START POINT: either by climbing *Manhattan* (page 76) on the lower buttress of the Grande Floria, or from the Index chairlift (page 95).
DIFFICULTY: D+, 6a, 5c oblig. Slabs. More of a mountain atmosphere than the other classics in the area. Generously bolted. *In situ* abseil stations.
TIMES: approach 20 mins from *Manhattan*, 50 mins from the chairlift; abseils 45 mins.
VERTICAL HEIGHT: approx. 200m.
CONDITIONS: snowfields on the approach at the beginning of the season. The face is quickly snow-free in spring and the route dries quickly after rain.
FIRST ASCENT: P. Dethurens, M. Piola & P. Strappazzon, 8 August 2006.

The Petite Floria is famous for its traverse via the Saint-Georges Gendarme. In contrast, *Kaboul*, on the steep south face, is a thoroughly modern climb, although with the added spice of a pristine setting and a ridge traverse below the summit, which add to the satisfaction of attaining an isolated peak with an outstanding view. Combined with *Manhattan*, the route becomes a much bigger undertaking that requires an efficient approach.

The first pitch is very steep but covered in holds (5b).

APPROACH

(a) From *Manhattan*: follow the finishing ledge westwards, then make a long rising traverse (scree or snow) to get to a slab of red rock below the left-side of the face. 20 mins.

(b) From the Index chairlift: traverse north-west across the foot of the Index snowfield. Go across the left-bank moraine and continue up the snow-field (or scree slope) below the western flank of the Grande Floria. Aim for the south face of the Petite Floria, which is separated from the Grande by a deep gully that holds the snow long into the season. Continue to the slab of red rock at the foot of the left-hand buttress. 45 mins.

START

Go up the red slab (2b, 40m) to the starting ledge, ring bolt, B0.

Notes: Between B2 and B3 it is possible to climb a lovely but stiff and quite strenuous 6c pitch: *Pensée Afghane* (35m, Fixe bolts).

At B4, look to the left of the belay in order to note landmarks for the descent (cairn).

DESCENT

From the summit, climb back down to B4 by looping round to the right (loose rock) to a cairn and then traversing left. From B4, do two abseils to the ledge at B2. Traverse back along the ledge (west) to B1, then do two more abseils to get to the foot of the red slab.

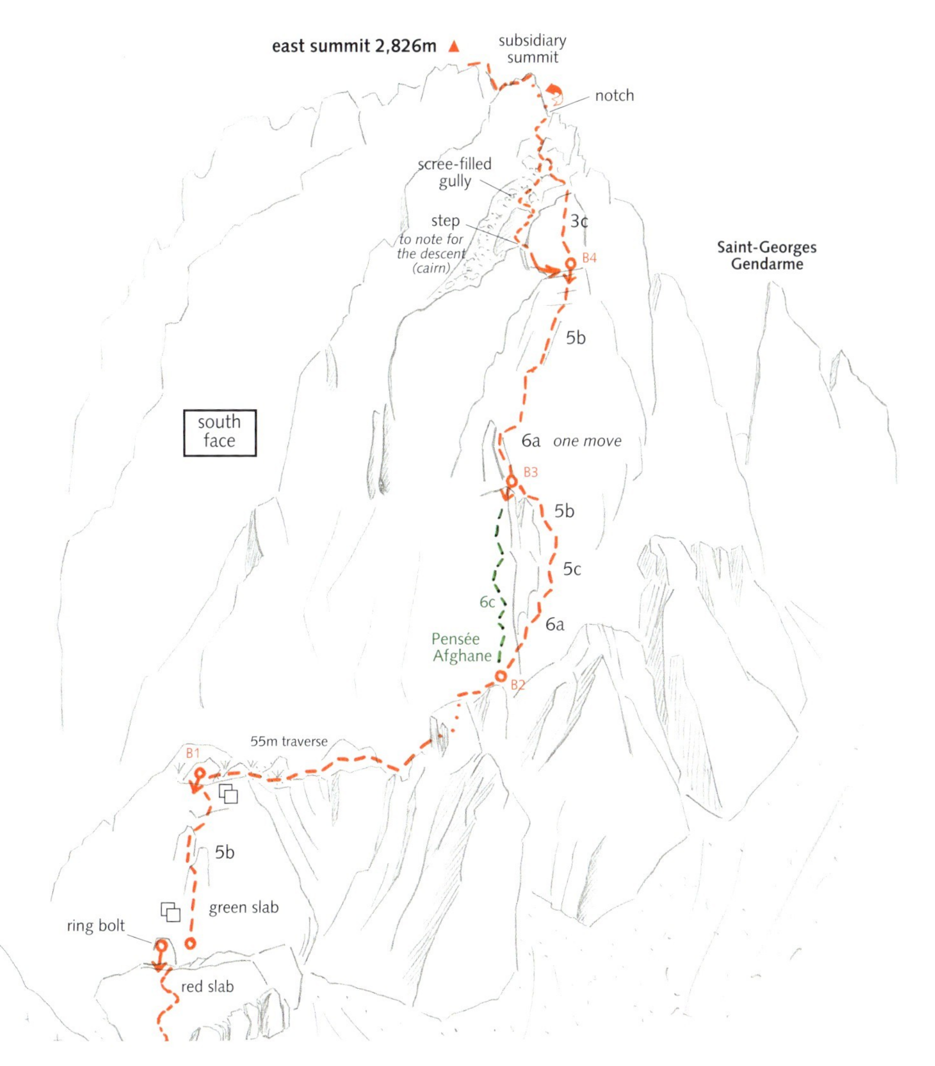

The Petite Floria, as seen from the approach.

AIGUILLE DE LA FLORIA (2,888M)

SOUTH FACE: MANHATTAN (KABOUL), ASIA, FRAISES DES BOÂTCHS

START POINT: top of the Index chairlift (2,396m), reached from La Flégère. See page 95.
TIMES: approach 20 mins; routes 2–3 hrs; descents 10 mins to 1 hr.
VERTICAL HEIGHTS: 200–400m.
CONDITIONS: the routes can seep when the snow is melting or after heavy rain.
GEAR: small nuts.
FIRST ASCENTS: *Manhattan*: P. Dethurens & M. Piola, 21 July 2006; *Asia*: M. Piola solo, 17 and 23 September 1995; *Fraises* ... : E. Méot, P.-A. de Potestad & J. Cellier, August 1999.

The lower buttress of the Grande Floria is criss-crossed with routes, allowing numerous combinations. *Asia*'s sustained series of pitches has made it one of the most popular climbs in the Aiguilles Rouges and traffic jams are common, so you will need to be quite crafty if you want to have the route to yourself.

On paper, *Fraises des Boâtchs* is the easiest route on the face, but the steepness and overlapping structure of the rock, together with the spaced bolts and the difficulty of placing nuts, give food for thought. It is also the only route that continues to the summit of the Grande Floria, high above the ship of fools.

The rock on *Manhattan* is bombproof. The route was always conceived as a lower section to *Kaboul*, on the Petite Floria, further up the mountainside (page 74).

APPROACH

From the chairlift, head north across the foot of the Index snowfield. Go over the left-bank moraine and traverse another snowfield to the foot of the buttress. 20 mins.

MANHATTAN (KABOUL)

TD-, 200m, 6a, 5c oblig. Slabs and overhanging walls. Bolted. Last two pitches criss-cross *Madagasikara*.

START

Approx. 50m left of the ramp that runs across the wall and to the left of the single-pitch crag at the foot of the buttress. It is the only route with resin bolts.

DESCENT

From the top of the first buttress:

- Three abseils down an independent line, slightly below and to the left of B5.
- Walk down: head west along the ledge, then go down the scree slope (or snowfield) on the left edge of the buttress.
- Continue up *Kaboul* (see page 74).

ASIA

D+, 250m, 6a, 5c oblig. Sustained series of pitches on steep gneiss. Requires good footwork, even on the overhanging start (6a or A0). Well bolted. Two sections with escape possible at the top of each.

START

Just to the right of the foot of the lower of two ramps that divide the lower buttress.

DESCENT

Either abseil down the independent abseil line or walk off (do not abseil down the route).

- From the top of the first buttress – see *Manhattan*.
- From the top of the second buttress – either climb down a short gully on the west side to get to the Index snowfield (40 mins), or go down the slopes to the east, then head south (50 mins).

FRAISES DES BOÂTCHS

D+, 400m, 5b oblig. Delicate slab climbing. Spaced gear on the lower buttress. Rock requires care in places.

START

50m to the right of *Asia*.

DESCENT

It is best not to abseil down the route (obstruct other climbers, stone-fall).

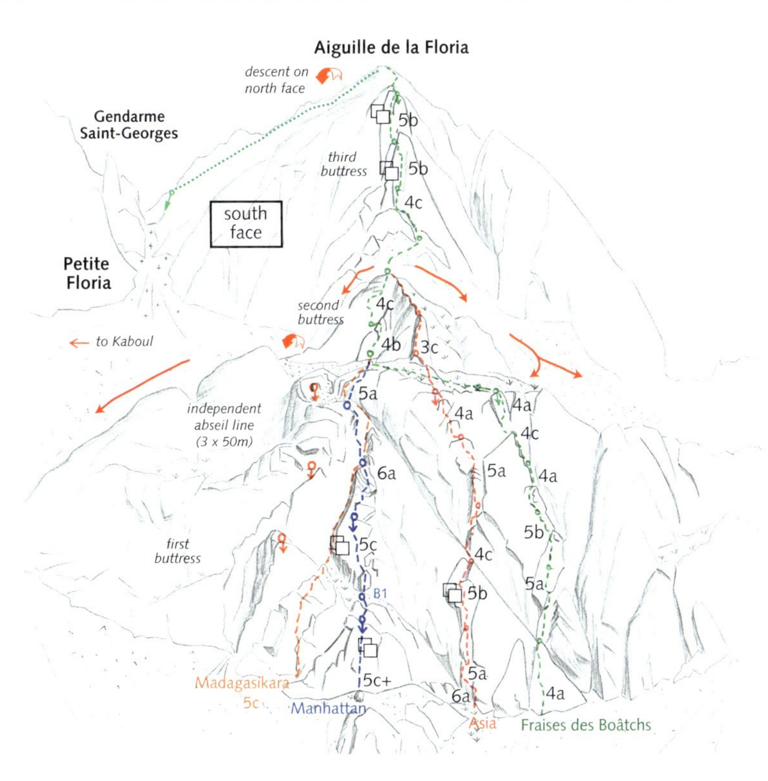

- From the top of the first buttress – see *Manhattan*.
- From the top of the second buttress – see *Asia*.
- From the summit of the Floria:

(a) Via the south-west ridge: go down the north face, just below the south-west ridge (scree), then traverse left to get back on the ridge above the gendarmes overlooking the Col Supérieur de la Floria. Continue down a gully and a short chimney (south-west). Descend the steep part of the snowy gully below the col via a 50m abseil from the foot of the chimney. Go down the rocks on the right bank of the snowfield to the Combe de l'Index. 1 hr.

(b) Climb down to the last belay, from where three abseils lead to the foot of the upper buttress. Walk down the slopes on the right (west, slightly shorter) or the left (east, then south-east) to get back to the Index (40–50 mins).

The Petite Floria: *Kaboul* (white line, see page 74)

POINTE GASPARD (2,741M)

SOUTH FACE: GASPARD 1ER, LADY IN BLACK

START POINT: top of the Index chairlift (2,396m), reached from La Flégère. See page 95.
TIMES: approach 30 mins; routes 2–3 hrs; descent 15–30 mins.
VERTICAL HEIGHTS: 170–200m.
CONDITIONS: south facing so dries quickly.
GEAR: nuts, cams 1–3 for *Gaspard 1er*.
FIRST ASCENTS: *Gaspard 1er*: S. Ravanel, 12 September 2001; *Lady in Black*: M. Piola & M. Rebetez, 11 September 2007.

How long does it take for a route to become a 'classic'? It depends on how frequently it is climbed, so it can take years. But now, in the internet age, word can get round at lightning speed, and some routes become classics in a matter of months. *Gaspard 1er* is one such route. With a lovely atmosphere and a good balance between difficulty and pleasure, it is definitely a route to do.

Lady in Black is another story. Threading a way through intimidating overhangs and with rock that will require many ascents to clean up, it is a much more exacting proposition. The pleasure is in working out the best line, unravelling the mystery as you climb, reliving the spirit of the pioneers who first explored our beautiful Alps.

GASPARD 1ER

D+, 200m, 5b+, 5a oblig. Classic slabs and a granite-style crack. Fully bolted.

APPROACH

Head north-east along the path (or across snowfields) from the top of the Index chairlift to pass below the right-hand buttress of the Grande Floria. Go across the Combe des Aiguilles Crochues, to the spur that extends below Pointe Gaspard into the scree slope. Go up the left edge of this spur for about 50m to the start of the route (obvious ledge, the first bolt – on the pillar above – is hard to see). 30 mins.

DESCENT

From the summit, head northwards down the ridge and go over the Col des Aiguilles Crochues (2,704m). Descend the gully on the south-east face (snowfield or path), then go back below the face to the Index chairlift. 25 mins.

Notes: The belays are equipped for an abseil descent but abseiling down the route takes longer and is more complicated than walking down via the Col des Aiguilles Crochues.

LADY IN BLACK

TD-, 170m, 6a oblig. Mostly slabs. Well bolted except for B4 (1 bolt). Complex route finding. Rock on the last two pitches requires care. Abseil down the route.

APPROACH

As for *Gaspard 1er*, but continue up the scree for another 50m to a ringbolt in a pink slab. This is the start of *Post. Lady in Black* starts a few metres further left (Raumer bolt hangers).

DESCENT

Abseil down the route.

Note: B4 currently has only one bolt, from which it is a 50m abseil to B2. Otherwise, follow the ridge eastwards towards the summit, then descend via the Col des Aiguilles Crochues.

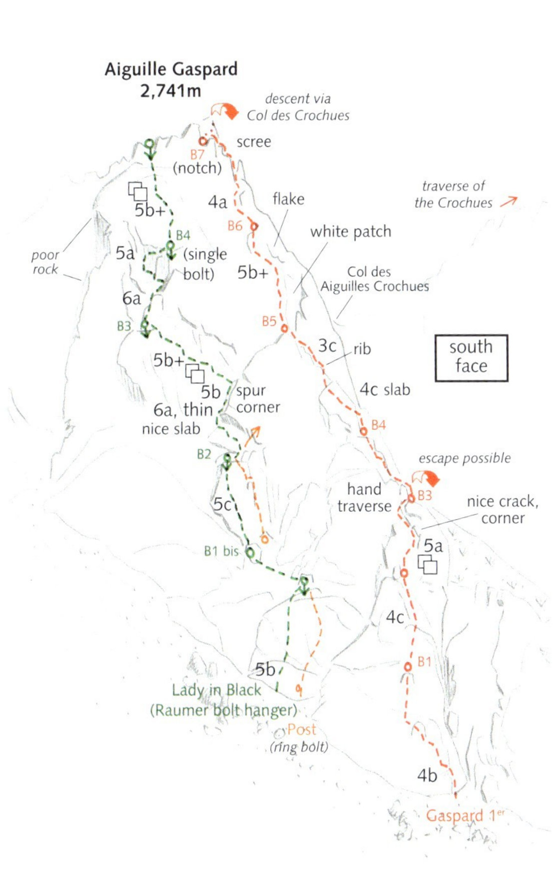

Above: P3 of *Lady in Black* (5b).

Below: Pic Gaspard with the Crochues to the right.

Opposite page: At the start of *Lady in Black* (5b).

AIGUILLES CROCHUES – SOUTH SUMMIT (2,840M)

SOUTH RIDGE: RAVANEL ROUTE

START POINT: top of the Index chairlift (2,396m). See page 95.
DIFFICULTY: TD- 6a, 5c oblig. Steep first section. Summit ridge less sustained (one move of 5+/6a or A0). Mountain atmosphere. Rock requires care in places. Well bolted, including the belays. Equipped for an abseil descent up to B7.
TIMES: approach 30 mins; route 4 hrs; descent 1 hr to get back to the Index.
VERTICAL HEIGHT: 400m.
CONDITIONS: sun at the foot of the pillar at around 9.30 a.m. in summer. The start of the route can be cold. The first pitch sometimes seeps after rain.
GEAR: 12 quickdraws, a few nuts.
FIRST ASCENT: G. Chapus & S. Ravanel, August 2003.

Sylvain Ravanel must have had his eye in to pick out such a homogenous line in the immensity of the south face. The Dolomitic ambience and a finish on the summit of the Crochues give this great route a true high-mountain feel.

APPROACH

Head north from the Index towards the Combe des Crochues, passing below the right-hand buttress of the Grande Floria. At the top of the snowfield, instead of going up towards the Col des Aiguilles Crochues, continue heading north-east along the almost horizontal wide track. At the Combe des Crochues, go up across the scree slope (or snowfield) towards the obvious Y-shaped gully. The route starts 30m to the left of this gully and just to the left of a black overhanging wall (first bolt can be seen 5m from the ground). 30 mins.

The smooth slab on P4 (5c).

DESCENT

From the summit, head north down stepped ledges for 50m. Follow the right flank of the south-west ridge to a shoulder above a notch with three gendarmes. Go round the first gendarme to get to the south side of the notch, then follow a ledge round the north side of the second gendarme. Move back on to the ridge by climbing an 8m corner (bolt at the top). Climb a few metres higher on to the crest of the now-wide ridge. Follow the north side of the ridge to the Col des Aiguilles Crochues (a chimney to descend, 3a). From the col, go down the south-west slopes beside Pic Gaspard (path) to the snowfield, then follow the approach route back to the Index chairlift.

The Ravanel Spur on the Aiguilles Crochues.

32

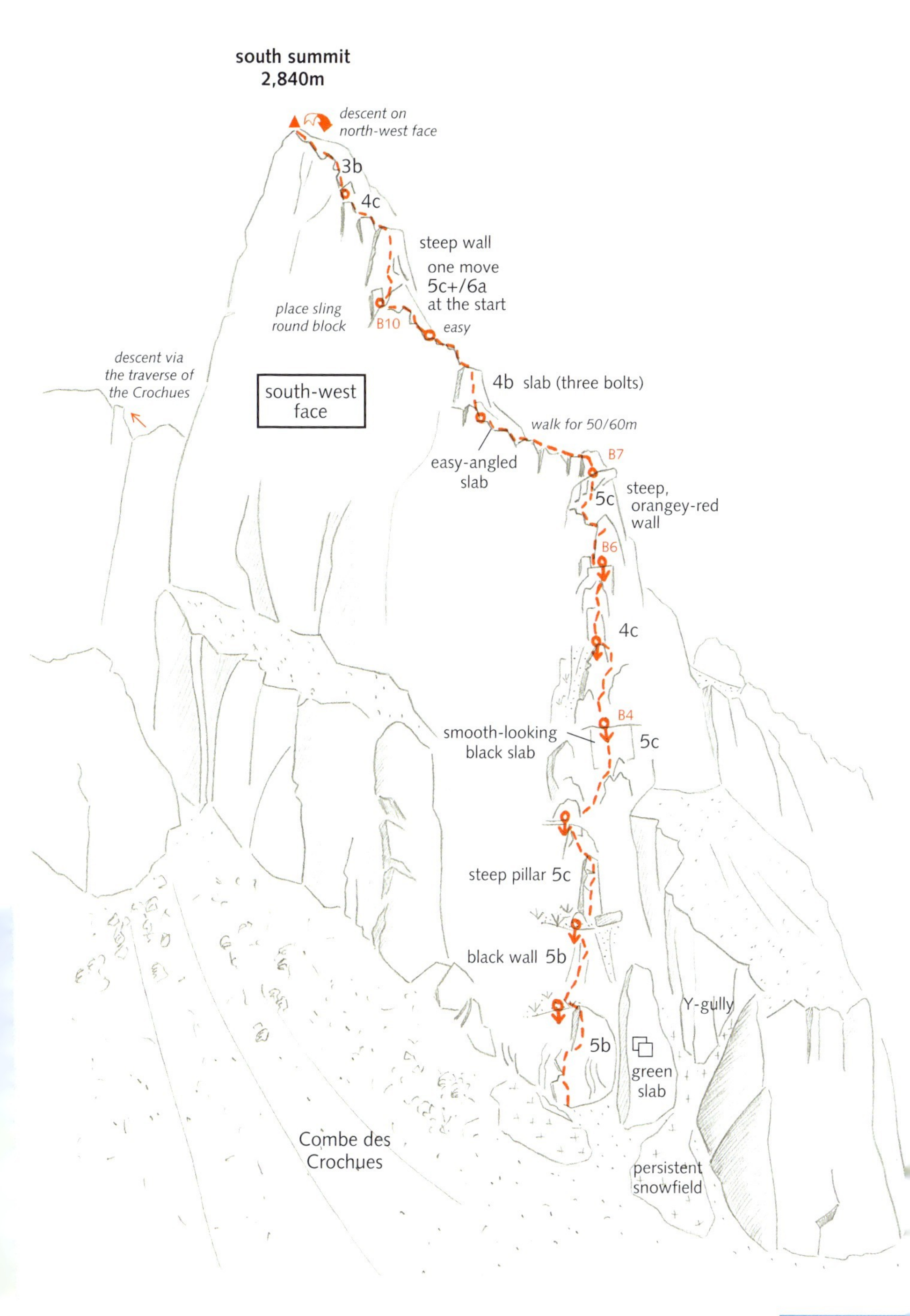
south summit
2,840m
descent on
north-west face
3b
4c
steep wall
one move
5c+/6a
at the start
place sling
round block
B10
easy
descent via
the traverse of
the Crochues
south-west
face
4b slab (three bolts)
walk for 50/60m
easy-angled
slab
B7
5c
steep,
orangey-red
wall
B6
4c
B4
smooth-looking
black slab
5c
steep pillar 5c
black wall 5b
Y-gully
5b
green
slab
Combe des
Crochues
persistent
snowfield

TOUR DES CROCHUES (2,589M)

SOUTH-WEST FACE: LES VIOLONS TZIGANES, DE GALBERT ROUTE

START POINT: top of the Index chairlift (2,396m) reached from La Flégère. See page 95.
TIMES: approach 45 mins, routes 2–3 hrs; descent 20 mins to the foot of the wall.
VERTICAL HEIGHT: 200m.
CONDITIONS: the face is steep and very sunny, so it is sometimes possible to climb here in winter. Can seep after rain. Sun at the end of the morning in summer.
GEAR: *Les Violons Tziganes*: 12 quickdraws, micro-nuts. *De Galbert Route*: cams 1–3.
FIRST ASCENTS: *Les Violons Tziganes*: J. Haeni, C. Levet & M. Piola, 9 March 2003 and 30 July 2004; *De Galbert Route*: D. Escande & P. de Galbert, 9 September 1970.

Thanks to a gargantuan cleaning effort and some obsessive sieges, eight routes sprouted on this grandiose face in just a few seasons. To get the most from these climbs, wait until the midday sun picks out the lines, highlights the colours and warms the muscles.

We chose *Les Violons Tziganes*, a modern middle-grade route, for its position centre-stage, its summit finish and its superb middle pitches.

The gneiss on the more traditional *De Galbert Route* holds several surprises, including its steepness, its sloping holds and its relative fragility. Grade-5 climbers used to climbing out-doors will delight in the big wall atmosphere.

APPROACH

From the Index, head north-east along the path to Lac Blanc. When the path descends to go across the Combe des Aiguilles Crochues, turn left and go up the scree slopes or snowfields in the middle of the cirque (north) to the foot of the wall. 45 mins.

During the approach, note the two large gullies to the right of the face. The descent takes the right-hand gully.

LES VIOLONS TZIGANES

TD, 6a+, 6a oblig. Sustained, steep and strenuous. Requires an ability to read the rock. P3 and P4 are a little bold (nuts and cams difficult to place). P5 is longer than 50m.

The route starts where the scree gives way to grass, at a black wall above a short green step (Fixe bolt hangers).

DESCENT

It is inadvisable to abseil down the route due to the risk of stone-fall and of obstructing other climbers. The descent via the gully to the east of the summit is quick and easy: from the summit follow the edge of the ridge south-eastwards (on the right) to an obvious saddle with a large cairn, 200m from the top of the route. Climb down the easy gully (west) to get back to the foot of the wall. 20 mins.

Retrace your steps back to the Index or go straight down to La Flégère: After heading south across the Lac Blanc path, follow the obvious combe below the Combe des Crochues (ski run) to a wide track. Follow this track (south-west) back to La Flégère. 1 hr.

DE GALBERT ROUTE

D+, 5c, 5b oblig. Some fragile rock. Complex route finding. Old pegs must be backed up with nuts and cams.

START

A few metres left of the top of the gorge at the right-hand edge of the wall.

DESCENT

See *Les Violons Tziganes*.

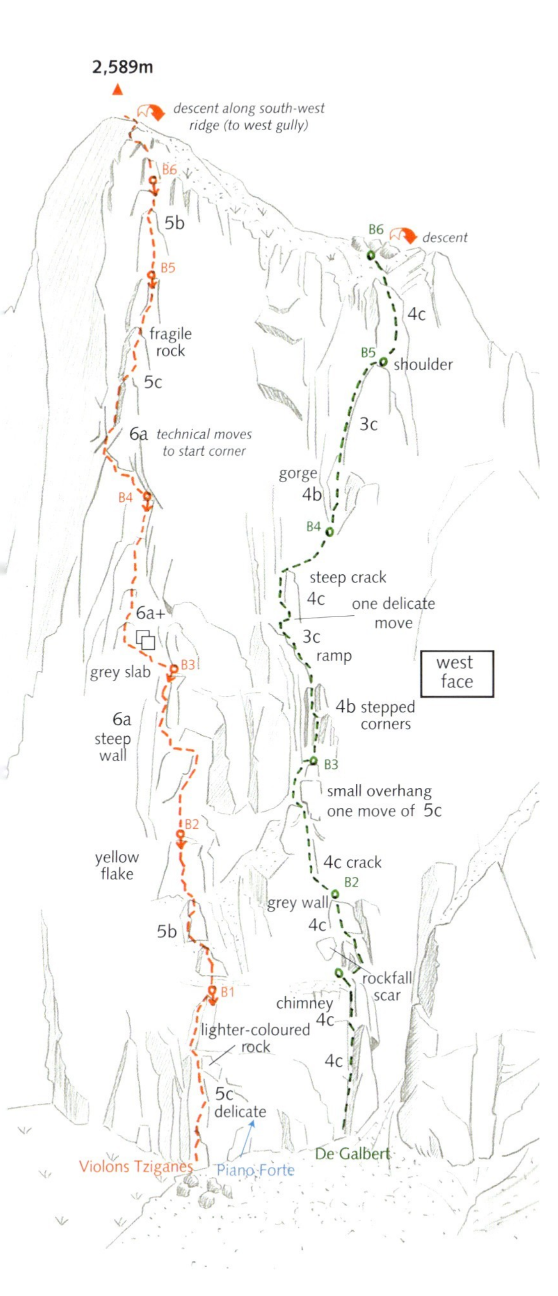

At the start of P5 (6a).

AIGUILLE DE PRAZ TORRENT (2,573M)

EAST FACE: PARAT-SEIGNEUR ROUTE

START POINT: La Poya car park, reached by going over the Col des Montets towards Vallorcine. 500m before the station at Le Buet, turn left on to the driveable track that leads to the Bérard waterfall. Park at the barrier.

DIFFICULTY: TD, 6a, 5c oblig. Varied. Steep and sometimes exposed. Complex route finding. Nuts and cams needed to complement *in situ* gear.

TIMES: approach 1½ hrs; climb 3 hrs; descent to the foot of the route 30 mins.

VERTICAL HEIGHT: 250m.

CONDITIONS: from spring to autumn, seeps after heavy rain.

GEAR: nuts, set of cams up to size 4 (for P8).

FIRST ASCENT: A. Parat & Y. Seigneur, 6 July 1969.

The approach is long, but the first sight of the face is sure to make you forget the sweat on your back. Take a break and try to pick out the line first climbed by the unstoppable team of André Parat and Yannick Seigneur. It is the unspoilt setting people come here to savour. Your forearms will be severely tested, as you overcome the succession of ramps, overhangs, corners, chimneys and parallel-sided cracks that lead to the final, easy ridge, climbed moving together, and the abseil into the descent gully.

APPROACH

Go past the barrier and follow the stony track to the ski lift. The path starts in the southern corner of the little car park and heads up southwards to a shoulder (1,803m, 1 hr). Follow a steep crest (west) to the left-hand side of the face. 1½ hrs.

START

At a rightward leaning ramp where the scree gives way to grass and the path reaches the cliff. The slings at the first belay can be seen by standing back slightly from the base of the cliff.

DESCENT

From the summit, follow the jagged ridge northwards for about 400m, at first on its left side and then on the right (intermittent path, slabs and ledges). When the ridge curves west, traverse left, descending slightly, then go up to an obvious notch and the abseil point. A 50m abseil down the west face leads to the top of the scree slope (or snowfield), which is followed back to the foot of the route.

The superb corner on P4 (4c).

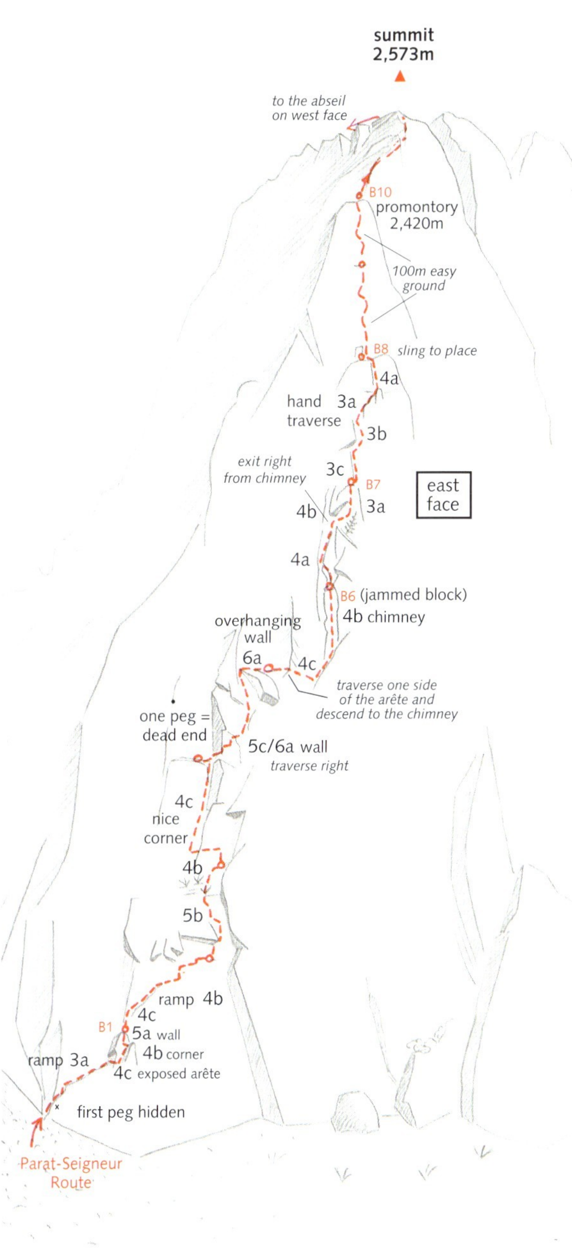

TÊTE DES MESURES (SPOT HEIGHT 1,981M)

NORTH-WEST BUTTRESS: L'ÎLE AUX RAZMOKETS

START POINT: La Poya car park, reached by going over the Col des Montets towards Vallorcine. 500m before the station at Le Buet, turn left on to the driveable track that leads to the Bérard waterfall. Park at the barrier.

DIFFICULTY: D-, 5b+, 5b oblig. Very well bolted slabs with *in situ* abseil stations. Unusual rock on P2. Frequently wet after B8.

TIMES: approach 1 hr; route 1¾ hrs to B8, 1 hr more to B12; abseils 40 mins to 1 hr.

VERTICAL HEIGHT: first section approx. 200m; upper buttresses approx. 100m.

CONDITIONS: dries slowly after rain, especially the upper section. Gets the sun in the middle of the day.

GEAR: nuts for the upper section.

FIRST ASCENT: S. Ravanel & R. Passy, 12 June 2001.

The huge slab of *Razmokets* has rapidly become a classic, a route everyone should do. Its appeal comes from the style of the climbing, always on the feet, never strenuous, and the well-placed bolts. Topping out from the upper buttresses, you emerge into a different and completely disconnected world.

Surrounded by larch trees and north facing, the route is agreeably cool on hot summer days. What is more, the idyllic stream at the foot of the slab, with its little beaches and tiny waterfalls, is a lovely place for a shady picnic.

APPROACH

From the car park, follow the track to the Bérard waterfall (20 mins). Continue along the Bérard valley path to spot height 1,528m (15 mins). Just before the bridge (rock bearing the no.16), turn off on to a faint (at first) path along the right bank of the stream. Follow this path for about 10 mins, then head south up the slope, bearing right to get to the foot of the route (1,600m). 1 hr from the car park.

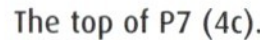

DESCENT

Abseil down the route.

The top of P7 (4c).

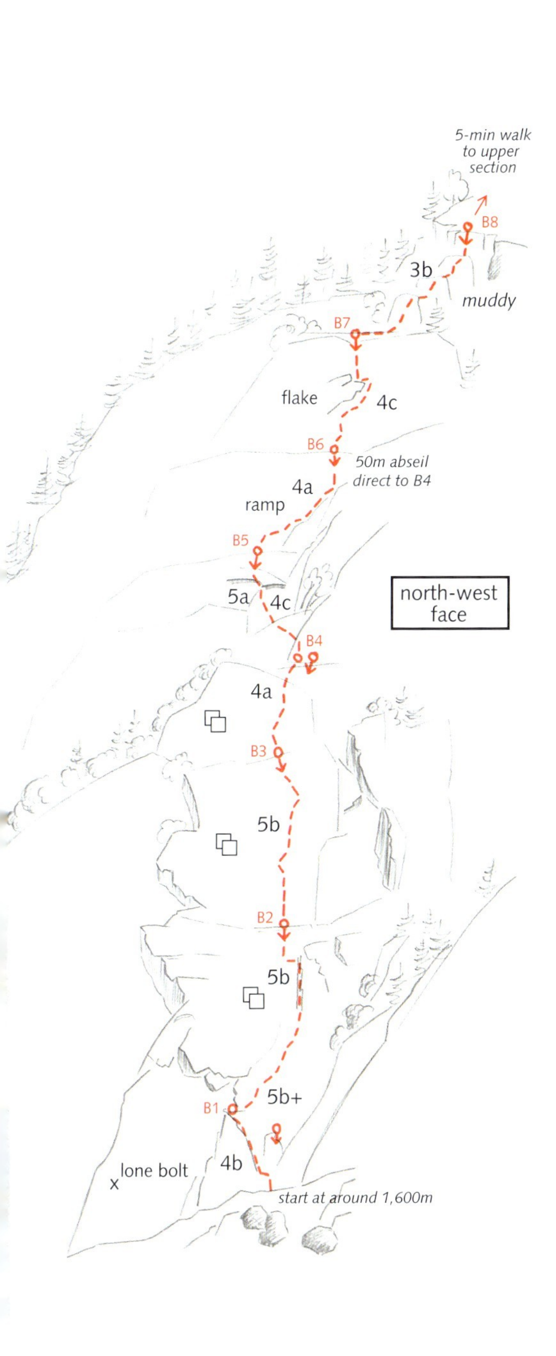

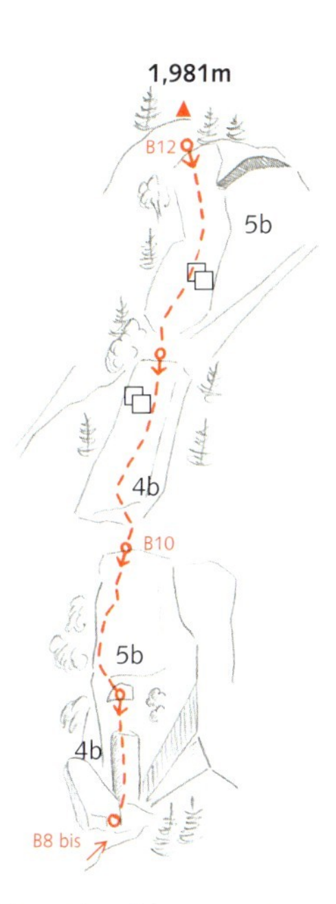

The four pitches of the upper section.

Above the overhang on P5.

MONT OREB (SPOT HEIGHT 2,100M)

SOUTH BUTTRESS: L'ÉTÉ INDIEN

START POINT: La Poya car park, reached by going over the Col des Montets towards Vallorcine. 500m before the station at Le Buet, turn left on to the driveable track that leads to the Bérard waterfall. Park at the barrier.

DIFFICULTY: TD-, 6a, 5c oblig. Delicate climbing on small edges. Sustained series of pitches. Well bolted. Abseil down the route.

TIMES: approach 1½ hrs; route 2 hrs; abseils 50 mins; return 1 hr.

VERTICAL HEIGHT: 230m.

CONDITIONS: steep wall so sheds snow quickly but it can seep after rain.

FIRST ASCENT: J. Mottin & H. Thivierge, October 2001.

When the summer season in the temple of mountaineering is at its height, it can be good to find an unspoilt corner in which to relax, a place where the rock is excellent and the pace less frenetic. The Bérard valley attracts hikers, who prudently stay on the waymarked trails, as well as climbers who are prepared to stray from the beaten track for more adventurous ground on which to test their mettle.

L'Été Indien combines solid and barely scuffed rock, intelligently placed bolts, flowing moves, and five-star belays – what more could you want?

APPROACH

From the car park, take the track to the Bérard waterfall (20 mins), then follow the path up the valley on the right bank of the stream. Cross the footbridge at 1,528m and continue up the left bank to a moraine plateau. A short distance along the plateau (spot height 1,702m, cairn, 1 hr 20 mins), turn right (north-west) on to the obvious path that leads to the foot of the route. 1½ hrs from the car park.

DESCENT

Abseil down the route.

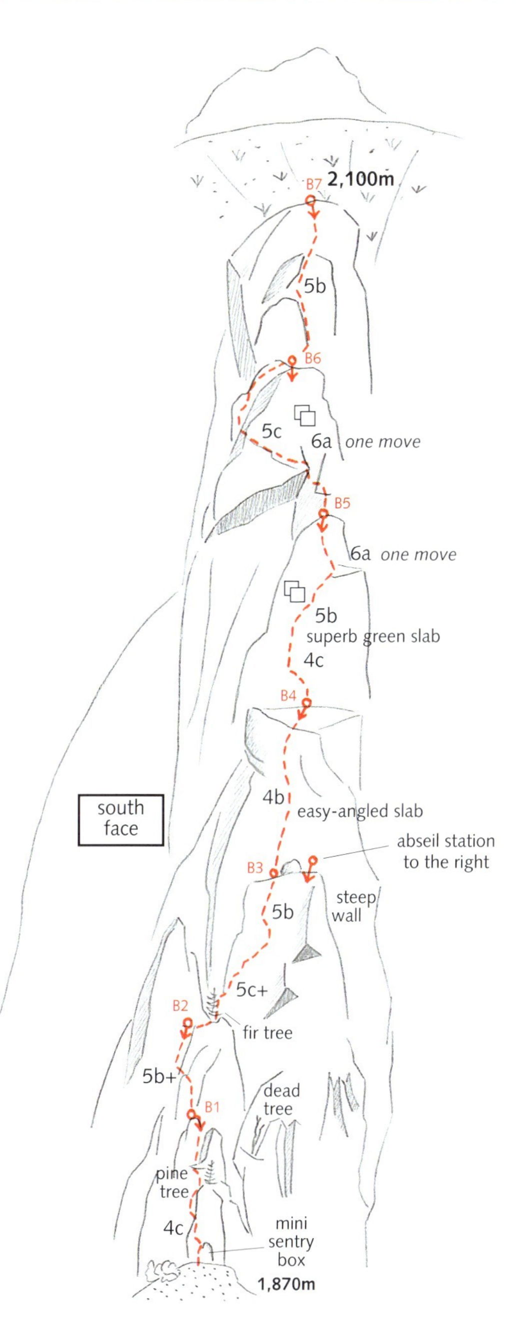

The obvious buttress of *L'Été Indien*, seen from spot height 1,702m.

Opposite page: At the top of the 5b slab.

The airy traverse on P6 (6a).

GRAND PERRON (2,673M)

SOUTH FACE: LA BALLADE DES GENS HEUREUX

START POINT: Émosson Dam (1,960m) in Switzerland, 43km from Chamonix via the Col des Montets.
DIFFICULTY: TD, 6a+, 6a oblig. Mostly slabs. Sustained series of pitches. One steep section (6a+ or A0) Spaced bolts. Compact rock – few nut or cam placements. *In situ* abseil stations.
TIMES: approach 1¾ hrs; route 3 hrs; abseils 1 hr; return to car park 1¼ hrs.
VERTICAL HEIGHT: 240m.
CONDITIONS: sunny aspect means the route quickly comes into condition in spring.
FIRST ASCENT: R. Bourdier, S. Ravanel & R. Passy, 9 and 15 October 1999.

The magnificent south face of the Grand Perron rises high above the Loriaz meadows, a peaceful place if ever there was one. Here, you are at the foot of a uniquely vast architectural complex whose numerous arched buttresses dictate the line of the route. Each section has to be deciphered metre by metre in order to progress between the well-spaced and difficult-to-see bolts, calling on finesse, subtlety, intuition and determination as your guides. What a route!

APPROACH

From the car park, follow the road across the dam for about 15 mins. Turn left (south) to go up a staircase carved out of a fallen tree trunk (signpost for *Loriaz, Barberine*). Two minutes later, turn south towards Loriaz. Follow this undulating footpath (waymarkers, chains) for another 45 mins to around 2,090m and the start of the path (on the right, west-north-west) to the cliff, which now comes into view. After another 10 mins, at around 2,150m, turn left on to a path through the rhododendrons and go up to a scree slope.

Cross the scree and head north-west up the grassy slope. Cross another slope of large boulders (cairns) and then scree to get to a snowfield. Go left round this snowfield to get to the start of the route. 1¾ hrs.

DESCENT

Abseil down the route.

The crux (6a+), in the middle of the immense south face.

PERRONS

Émosson Reservoir seen from the summit.

The final abseil.

BARBERINE (1,500M)

SOUTH FACE: SYLVIE PHOBIE

START POINT: Barberine, village on the Swiss border, after the Col des Montets. 20km from Chamonix.
DIFFICULTY: TD+, 6b+, 6a oblig. Smooth slabs with a few overhangs. Fully bolted.
TIMES: approach 20 mins; route 2½ hrs; abseils 45 mins.
VERTICAL HEIGHT: 250m.
CONDITIONS: sunny aspect, snow melts quickly but the slabs can stay damp after rain.
FIRST ASCENT: F. Oms, R. Passy & S. Ravanel, 1993.

It is great to have a low-lying crag for days of uncertain weather. At Barberine, you can choose between single-pitch routes and ten-pitch routes that you can abseil off at any time. If you are fascinated by the mysteries of friction climbing, it is the place to go. *Sylvie Phobie* is the most homogeneous route on the crag and the best bolted, although you might need a pair of wings as you near the summit ... Just go for it!

APPROACH

From the car park, head north-west through the village. After the last house, turn right (north) on to a narrow path through a meadow. Cross the bridge over the stream, then bear left and follow a faint path through the woods to a scree slope. Head leftwards up the scree (cairns) to the foot of the route, hidden among the fir trees (*Sylvie Phobie* inscribed on a metal plaque). 20 mins.

Sylvie Phobie climbs a perfect dome.

Smearing above Barberine.

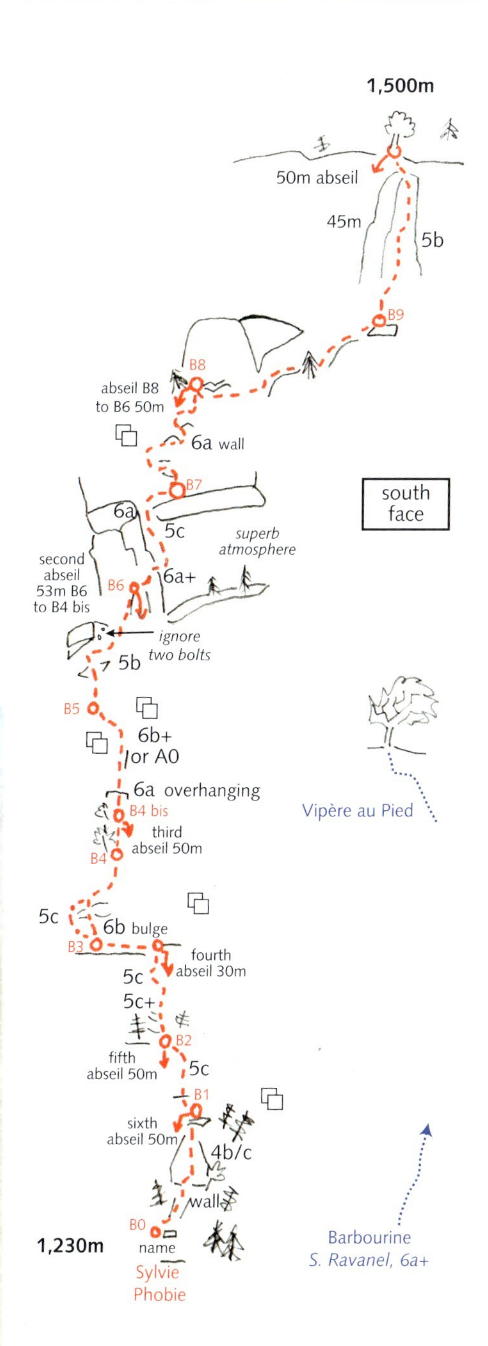

The outstanding seventh pitch – not a positive hold in sight!

HUTS, LIFTS & INFORMATION

HUTS

- Booking obligatory.
- Access descriptions are designed to be used in conjunction with the 1:25,000-scale IGN Top 25 map for Chamonix (3630 OT).

GPS points: UTM format, WGS 84 system.
Climbers should also carry and know how to use a compass and altimeter.

- Abbreviations CAF, CAI, CAS: French, Italian and Swiss Alpine Clubs.

ALBERT PREMIER (1ER) HUT (2,702M)

Tel. 0033 (0)450540620. Staffed in summer and some spring weekends. CAF. 150 places.
Start point: village of Le Tour (20km north of Chamonix).
Access: take the Charamillon-Balme ski lifts to the Col de Balme, then follow a good path that trends south-east then south across the hillside. At around 2,330m, below the Bec du Picheu, turn left (east) and cross an area of scree (or snow), then continue up to the hut. 1½ hrs (4 hrs if you don't take the lifts to the Col de Balme).
GPS 32T E 0344 117 N 5095 662

ARGENTIÈRE HUT (2,771M)

Tel. 0033 (0)450531692. Staffed in summer and from February to May. CAF. 140 places. Glacier approach.
Start point: Argentière, Grands Montets cable car.
Access: from the top cable car station, go down to the Col des Grands Montets (3,233m). Cross the bergschrund and head north-east down the Glacier des Rognons to the top of the moraine (2,754m). Follow the crest of the moraine to the Glacier d'Argentière. Head south-east up the left bank of the glacier to around 2,700m, then traverse east to the right-bank moraine. The hut is 70m above the glacier. 1½ hrs.
GPS 32T E 0345 345 N 5090 015

COSMIQUES HUT (3,613M)

Tel. 0033 (0)450544016. Staffed from February to October. Private. 148 places. Glacier approach, exposed ridge.
Start point: Chamonix Sud, Aiguille du Midi cable car.
Access: from the top cable car station (3,795m) go down the north-east ridge (exposed) to the plateau at 3,605m. Go down the snow slopes below the south face of the Aiguille du Midi, bearing south at first and then south-west. Go up slightly to the hut. 20 mins.
GPS 32T E 0335 896 N 5082 115

DALMAZZI (2,590M) 'TRIOLET' HUT – ITALY

www.rifugiodalmazzi.com
Tel. 0039 (0)165 869098. Staffed from early July to September. CAI. 32 places. Perched on a grassy saddle above the left bank of the Glacier de Triolet, at the foot of the Monts Rouges. Access via moraine and small cliffs with *in situ* hand lines.
Start point: Arnouva (1,769m), at the end of the Italian Val Ferret, reached via the Mont Blanc Tunnel.
Access: from the car park, continue along the rocky road (signposted *refuge Elena*) for about 500m (15 mins). At the first right-hand bend (yellow sign at 1,860m: *Dalmazzi* 2¼ hrs), go down a narrow path on the left (north) and cross the braided stream via four successive footbridges. Go up boulder-strewn grassy slopes, then head north-west along the well signposted path (yellow waymarkers) on the crest of the moraine (45 mins from the car park) to a plateau at around 2,020m. The Parete dei Titani, home to *Génépi I* and *II* (chapter 21) and *Vénus*, can be seen on the right. At the top of the moraine (around 2,270m, large snow or scree slope), head due north up the grassy spur between two gullies for about 200m (fixed ropes), then traverse west below the cliffs under the hut. The path to the hut swings round westwards then eastwards (some metal ladders). 2½ hrs from the car park.
GPS 32T E 0348 000 N 5084 162

ENVERS DES AIGUILLES HUT (2,523M)

Tel. 0033 (0)676526117. Staffed from late June to mid-September. CAF. 60 places.
Perched on a rocky promontory at the foot of the south-east spur of the Aiguille de Roc. Glacier and ladders.
Start point: Chamonix, Montenvers-Mer de Glace station.
Access: from Montenvers (1,913m), climb down the ladders to the Mer de Glace. Go up the glacier to around 1,950m, then head south to the left-bank moraine and the foot of the ladders at the start of the path (white square on the rock). Contour round the mountainside, then go up a few switchbacks to traverse below the Glacier de Trélaporte. Head west up an area of steeper ground to go round the south face of the promontory below the hut. Go up and head back right to the hut. 2½ hrs.
GPS 32T E 0339 255 N 5085 025

ORNY HUT (2,811M) – SWITZERLAND

Tel. 0041 (0)277831887. Staffed from June to September. CAS. 80 places.
Lies above the left bank of the Glacier d'Orny.
Start point: Champex (Switzerland), La Breya chairlift.
Access: from the top of the chairlift (Grands Plans, 2,188m), head south-west along the path to the middle of the Combe d'Orny. Go up the valley (west) past the lake, then follow the moraine on the left bank of the glacier to the hut. 2 hrs.
GPS 32T E 0349 975 N 5096 075

TORINO HUT (3,371M) – ITALY

Summer hut: Tel. 0039 (0)165 844034. Staffed from June to September. CAI. 160 places.
Winter hut: Tel. 0039 (0)165 846484. Staffed in October and from December to June. 40 places.
Start point and access: from Italy, take the Funivie Monte Bianco cable car from La Palud (Italian Val Ferret) to the top station. The winter hut is at the station, from where an underground staircase leads to the summer hut (10 mins). From France, take the Aiguille du Midi and cross the Vallée Blanche on foot (glacier, 2½ hrs) or by the Panoramic Mont-Blanc gondola.
GPS 32T E 0339 548 N 5078 930

TRIENT HUT (3,170M) – SWITZERLAND

Tel. 0041 (0)277831438. Staffed in spring and summer. CAS. 150 places.
Start point: Champex (Switzerland), La Breya chairlift.
Access: from the top of the chairlift (Grands Plans, 2,188m), head south-west along the path to the middle of the Combe d'Orny. Go up the valley (west) past the lake, then follow the moraine on the left bank of the glacier to the Orny Hut (2 hrs). Continue along the left bank of the glacier to the Col d'Orny (3,098m), then head north to the hut (easy rocks, 1 hr). The hut can also be reached by following the good path on the right before the col (at around 3,000m). 3 hrs.
GPS 32T E 0348 517 N 5095 850

LIFTS

Operations are seasonal. Information about opening dates and times can be found at: www.chamonix.com or www.compagniedumontblanc.fr

AIGUILLE DU MIDI

Tel. 0033 (0)450533080
Starts in Chamonix-Sud. Two-stage cable car – midway station at the Plan de l'Aiguille (2,310m), top station at the Aiguille du Midi (3,795m). Possible to continue to Pointe Helbronner, in Italy, via the Panoramic Mont-Blanc gondola.

BRÉVENT

Tel. 0033 (0)450531318
Starts in Chamonix-Nord. Two-stage cable car – midway station at Planpraz (2,000m), top station on the summit of the Brévent (2,525m).

CHARAMILLON – BALME

Tel. 0033 (0)450540058
Starts in the village of Le Tour, 12km north-east of Chamonix, gondola to Charamillon (1,912m), then chairlift to just south of the Col de Balme (around 2,180m).

FLÉGÈRE – INDEX

Tel. 0033 (0)450531858
Starts in the village of Les Praz (2km north of Chamonix), cable car to La Flégère (1,877m), then chairlift to the Index (2,396m).

HELBRONNER – FUNIVIE MONTE BIANCO

Tel. 0039 (0)165 89 925 – www.montebianco.com
Starts in La Palud in Italy (15km from Chamonix via the Mont Blanc Tunnel).
Three-stage cable car – midway station at Le Pavillon-Mont Fréty (2,174m), top station at the Torino huts (3,322m). The final stage goes to the summit of Pointe Helbronner (3,462m), above the Col du Géant. Possible to continue to the Aiguille du Midi via the Panoramic Mont-Blanc gondola.

LA BREYA

Tel. 0041 (0)277831344
Starts in Champex in Switzerland (20km south of Martigny), chairlift to Les Grands Plans (2,188m).

LOGNAN – GRANDS MONTETS

Tel. 0033 (0)450540071
Starts 1km south of the village of Argentière (Chamonix Valley). Two-stage cable car – midway station at Croix de Lognan (1,973m), top station at Les Grands Montets (3,295m).

MONTENVERS – MER DE GLACE

Tel. 0033 (0)450531254
Rack and pinion railway from Chamonix (next to the SNCF railway station) to Montenvers (1,913m).

INFORMATION

OHM (OFFICE DE HAUTE MONTAGNE)

Place de l'Église, Chamonix. Tel. 0033 (0)450532208
www.ohm-chamonix.com

CHAMONIX TOURIST OFFICE

Tel. 0033 (0)450530024 – www.chamonix.com

LES HOUCHES TOURIST OFFICE

Tel. 0033 (0)450555062 – www.leshouches.com

SAINT-GERVAIS TOURIST OFFICE

Tel. 0033 (0)450477608 – www.st-gervais.net

CAF HUTS IN THE MONT BLANC RANGE

Tel. 0033 (0)450531603

WEATHER

FRENCH WEATHER SERVICE

Tel. 32 50 – www.meteo.fr

HAUTE-SAVOIE WEATHER BY TELEPHONE

Tel. (0)892680274

AOSTA VALLEY WEATHER SERVICE

www.regione.vda.it

ALPES ROMANDES WEATHER SERVICE

Tel. (0)41 848 800162
www.meteosuisse.ch

RESCUE SERVICES

INTERNATIONAL EMERGENCY NUMBER FROM A MOBILE PHONE

France 112 – Italy 118 – Switzerland 144

PGHM (PELOTON DE GENDARMERIE DE HAUTE MONTAGNE)

Chamonix: Tel. 0033 (0)4 50 53 16 89
Saint-Gervais: Tel. 0033 (0)4 50 78 10 81

BIBLIOGRAPHY

Mountaineering in the Mont Blanc Range: Classic Snow, Ice & Mixed Climbs
Jean-Louis Laroche & Florence Lelong (Vertebrate Publishing, 2014)

Mont Blanc: The Finest Routes
Philippe Batoux (Vertebrate Publishing, 2013)

Sommets du Mont-Blanc: Les plus belles courses de Facile à Difficile
Jean-Louis Laroche & Florence Lelong (Glénat, 1996)

Ascensions au Pays du Mont-Blanc
Jean-Louis Laroche & Florence Lelong (Glénat, 2000)

Snow, Ice and Mixed (two volumes)
François Damilano (JMEditions, 2005 and 2006)

Mont-Blanc Massif: Envers des Aiguilles
Michel Piola (2007)

Face au Mont-Blanc: Les Aiguilles Rouges
Michel Piola (2008)

L'Escalade: de la salle aux grandes parois rocheuses
Philippe Brass (Glénat, 2008)

On the lower buttress of the Floria, looking across to the Aiguille Verte.

INDEX OF CLIMBS (OVERALL DIFFICULTY AND OBLIGATORY RATING)

ALPHABETICAL INDEX OF SUMMITS

The routes included in this guidebook are presented for information only. Every mountaineer is responsible for his or her own decisions. Choices must take into account one's abilities and the risks arising from the conditions in the mountains. The route descriptions are accurate for the conditions and date on which they were climbed; however, climbers should check that a chosen route has not changed in any way, for example, due to rock-fall, glacial retreat or removal of *in situ* gear. The authors, editors and publishers cannot be held responsible for any accidents that occur on any of the routes described in this guidebook. As the guidebook is not updated at frequent intervals, it cannot be considered expert testimony in a court of law.

SAFETY STATEMENT

Climbing and mountaineering are activities that carry a risk of personal injury or death. Participants must be aware of and accept that these risks are present and they should be responsible for their own actions and involvement. Nobody involved in the writing and production of this guidebook accepts any responsibility for any errors that it contains, nor are they liable for any injuries or damage that may arise from its use. Climbing and mountaineering are inherently dangerous and the fact that individual descriptions in this volume do not point out such dangers does not mean that they do not exist. Take care.